ISABEL'S
HAND-ME-DOWN
DREAMS

What People Are Saying

"This is a delightful...evocative and exact depiction of people, place and time. The overall result is life-enhancing, a triumph of (Latin) spirit over adversity." Nick Poole, *The Shattered Mirror*

"An absolutely heartrending, gut-wrenching, beautiful memoir. The devastating feelings a young girl experiences at the hands of an alienated, abusive mother are rendered (and received) with powerful, undeniable emotion." Thomas Winton, *Beyond Nostalgia*

"I lost myself in this and became totally immersed in Isabel's world. It is beautifully written, and in places it reminded me of Angela's Ashes in the way I could hear, see and almost taste her New York." Patrick Fox, *Trinity*

"Her memories bring a real sense of time and place. I hear echoes of her mother's voice and smell the raindrops as they hit the sun-baked earth. I can see the Crayola colours and feel the cotton prints. The voices of her family will haunt that Manhattan tenement forever." Barry Harden, *Throwaway*

"Some memoirs are difficult to read because they're filled with such anger and sorrow. That's what makes this stand out: a sense of humor maintained in the face of terrific odds. A good read." Anthony Burgio, *Grain of Salt*

Isabel's Hand-Me-Down Dreams

Isabel López

To Aimée and Daniel

"Whether I shall turn out to be the hero
of my own life, or whether that station
will be held by anybody else,
these pages must show."
~Charles Dickens~

Contents

1

Coming to Nueva York

Plop! Plop! Plop! The raindrops fell one by one on the tin can my mother had placed outside her bedroom window as the cloudburst dwindled to a dripping trickle. It was the sound that lulled me to sleep as I snuggled under the covers, my mother lying next to me. Mother said it reminded her of the soothing rain dripping on Grandma's tin roof in Puerto Rico. It was the very same thought that came to mind, how the hypnotic mantra of raindrops percussing on tin could bring such calm, even though we were no longer under Abuela's roof.

What brought us to the mainland was all supposition since my mother always had a knack for stretching the truth. But the story that Mother most often told was that her mother-in-law was a *"bruja,"* a despicable witch who, for some reason, disliked my mother and made her life a living hell.

So, in the winter of 1954, my mother abruptly decided to move to New York. With my sister and me bundled in secondhand blankets and our grandmother in tow, she boarded a plane for a new life in New York City, without my father. I was two years old and my sister Wanda was one, too young to understand why we were being uprooted and too little to solidify our native roots.

I vaguely remember being carried off the plane, rain drizzling all around us, pitter patter on the wet concrete pavement. I couldn't feel the cold, had no concept of where I was, but I could hear the rain, and I felt safe.

Our first home was a teeming tenement on 106th Street and First Avenue, an area then inhabited mostly by Italian and Russian immigrants. The apartment was on the top floor of a six-floor walk-up, a one-bedroom railroad flat with the living room windows facing the backyard.

At night, I could see into the apartments across the litter-strewn courtyard and watch people going about their daily lives, following them from one room to another. Sometimes I would see things little girls should not be exposed to, but in my innocence, I wondered why people would want to dance so fitfully and naked at that.

The living room opened into the kitchen area and the main entryway. There in a corner was the multi-purpose bathtub—a place to bathe, wash clothes, scrub the cat, and defeather the doomed live chickens that Grandma brought home from *el vivero*. Next was a small bedroom which I sometimes shared with my mother, while Wanda and Grandma slept in the living room.

At the very end was a small rectangular room with a toilet, the kind you flush by pulling a chain from a box above it. This room became my haven away from all the noise and distractions, a place where I could lock myself in and spend hours reading books and fantasizing about being anywhere else.

I would meticulously cut out pictures from old books and magazines of places that seemed as unreal to me as my existence and, using moistened flour as glue, pasted them up all over the bathroom walls.

"Isabel, get out! What the hell are you doing in there?" Mother would yell, pounding on the door and disrupting my reverie.

The cold weather and the snow never made an impact on my sister and me as it was all we knew. But it surely must have affected my mother and grandmother, having left the exquisite beauty of a tropical island paradise for this cold and gray city where few spoke their language or understood where we came from.

Still, there was the rain, the memory of the pitter patter on a tin roof, the splashing of raindrops on flamboyan trees, the gushing of a heavy downpour on a wooden balcony floor that must have brought a familiar comfort to these remote surroundings.

"*Dios mio*, it's freezing cold here! What's wrong with that *cabron* super that he can't fix that boiler and give us some heat?" With that, my mother would take a large metal utensil and hit the radiator with forceful clangs. Soon, others in the building followed suit, and before long, they were communicating with each other in a Morse code of angry clamor.

"Isabel, Wanda, put on your coats and gloves and sit here," Grandma would beckon, placing chairs in front of the oven she had fired up. It was how we spent most of the winter months, huddled around the warmth of the hearth that Grandma created on frigid days.

I didn't know a word of English, and suddenly one day, I was left in a roomful of children who spoke a language I didn't understand. But it soon became great fun being around other kids, as my only playmate up to that point was my sister, Wanda. There must be a universal language among children that allowed me to quickly make friends, and every day I looked forward to crossing the threshold of that gloomy apartment into a world of fun games, finger painting, and funny songs I had learned phonetically.

I easily gravitated towards a little girl who spoke Spanish, just like me. Maria, a skinny, brown-sugared bilingual moppet, became my best friend, translator, and cultural attaché. With her help, I quickly learned the language so that by the time I graduated six years later, I knew enough English to be chosen class valedictorian.

Public School 168 was a daunting Victorian structure with arched windows on the top floors. All of the classrooms had wooden floors and matching wooden desks with attached bench seats, their ornate iron legs bolted to the floor. On the upper corner of each desk was an empty inkwell where we hid chewed wads of Bazooka bubble gum.

At 10:00 a.m., the teacher would hand out cartons of milk, and one could buy chocolate chip cookies for a penny each. Lunchtime was a nightmare, for the food they put on the trays was mostly unrecognizable and inedible.

The assistant principal at PS 168 was a towering wicked witch with a beak for a nose, who forced kids to eat every morsel on their trays. Everyone was morbidly afraid of her.

Feeling sorry for me, Grandma began to sneak in food from home during noon recess in the open courtyard. One day, she and I were crouched in a secluded corner of the schoolyard while I devoured a delicious homemade soup, when who should appear like a nightmare but the evil she-devil.

"What are you doing here, and who is SHE?" growled the towering behemoth with hands on hips.

"She eez my Grandma," I stammered nervously.

"Out! Tell her to leave now and don't ever do this again!" she said, crooked finger pointing toward the street.

"*Que dice*, Isabel?" What is she saying?

"Grandma, she says you can't bring me food anymore and she wants you to leave."

"*Ay, pero* Isabel, tell her you don't like the food here and you will starve if I can't bring you food."

"Young lady, I'm waiting!" thundered the witch, her black eyes shining like opals inside her gaunt face.

"Grandma, *está bien*. I will be okay. Just go home," I pleaded with Grandma, tears brimming.

Having waited long enough, the shrew forcefully picked me up by the arm, dragged me back to the cafeteria, and made me swallow a peanut butter and jelly sandwich. I hated the smell of peanut butter for a long time after that.

In school, I discovered the magic of books and became obsessed with reading, not for the sense of scholarly achievement, but because they kindled my imagination and transported me to places I could only dream of.

I read anything I could get my hands on, and there, in my self-decorated cavern with a toilet for a seat, I would spend hours reading, fascinated by other peoples' lives while trying to escape my own.

Mother was completely impervious to our little accomplishments. I often found myself waiting excitedly for her to come home so I could show her my papers with little stars glued on the top for a job well done, hoping for a compliment that never came. Eventually, I stopped showing her my work and used the stars to decorate the bathroom wall.

2

Abuela

G randma, or Mamá as we lovingly called her, was a petite woman with skin like silky light chocolate. When
she laughed, her gentle brown eyes became slits and her little pot belly would roll like Jell-O. She always wore her dark
hair brushed back in a mini-French roll with combs holding
it in place.

Her gentle features spoke silent words of kindness and
warmth and motherly love. Yet if you looked deep into her
eyes, you could almost see the tears she no longer shed.

Grandma was born in 1900 in the town of San Germán,
Puerto Rico, a historic treasure perched high on green
mountains on the southwest region of the island. Known
for its old-world Spanish architecture and the oldest church
in the western hemisphere, San Germán has streets so
steeply inclined that looking down from the top feels like
standing on a mountain's vertiginous summit. In the center
of town, narrow cobblestone streets are lined with pastel-

painted colonial homes, their ornate balconies beautifully decorated with plants and rainbow-colored flowers.

Hidden in the rural countryside are the shantytowns where people once lived in wooden shacks on stilts, some without electricity or running water. Barefoot children in tattered clothes ran amok on dirt streets playing make-believe games.

Poor and with little formal education, most of the men worked on farms or the sugar cane fields while the women sewed and ironed for a wage and cared for their children. It was there, in an area called Pueblo Nuevo, where my grandmother was born.

As a young girl, Grandma learned her mother's trade and began to earn a living making clothes with patches of fabric, which she artfully created on her hand-driven sewing machine.

In her mid-teens, she fell in love with Ramon who, like his father, worked in the sugar cane fields. Rebelling against her strict upbringing, she left her home to start a new life with Ramon, and together, they had seven children.

I loved listening to Grandma tell stories about her youth and growing up on the island. She once recounted with great sadness how she lost a child to dysentery, a disease that affected many children in those days.

"Back then, poor people relied on herbal remedies because medicines and doctors were scarce and expensive," she told me. "Many of us went to the local *curandera* for remedies. My baby boy was suffering from fevers and diarrhea, so I took him to the healer who gave me some herbal teas to give him.

"One day, while trying to give him the tea, he had a convulsion and fell limp in my arms. He never woke up."

"Oh, Mamá, how sad!"

"Yes, Isabel. We did the best we could and the rest we left up to God's will," she said with resignation.

"But Mamá, you had seven children, and five are living. What happened to the other one?"

"*Ay mi'ja*, my oldest boy was always getting into mischief, like your mother. I had forbidden him from playing in the fields where animals could be found scurrying in the trash that people threw there. One day, he didn't come home for supper, and I went crazy looking for him.

"I didn't know it then, but he had cut himself in the field and was afraid to come home. The following day, my neighbor found his body underneath my house in a pool of blood. *Ay*, Isabel, it wasn't easy raising children while working day and night for a pittance."

After bearing her seventh child, Grandma got wind of Ramon's infidelities. Eventually, he left her for another woman. Mamá carried on raising her five remaining children alone, never again to replace the love of her life.

The early 1950s saw a mass exodus of Puerto Ricans to the states, primarily because of the promise of jobs, living wages, and better living conditions. Word was getting back to the island that opportunities for a better life were abundant in America, prompting families to leave the homeland by the droves.

As United States citizens, Puerto Ricans traveled without legal encumbrances to the mainland, many settling in a section of Manhattan that would come to be known as "El Barrio." There, they slowly sought to recreate the familiar comforts of the island, with bodegas and markets sprouting like mango shoots from the asphalt turf.

On Saturday mornings, with a metal shopping cart in hand and a few dollars rolled in her dress pocket, Grandma and I would walk the two miles to La Marqueta, a noisy, swarming, outdoor and indoor marketplace where one could buy anything from socks to plungers. We would rummage through sidewalk boxes of calico fabrics and flowered prints that would eventually become a patchwork dress for me or Wanda.

We would then push our way through the crowded caboose-like indoor markets, past vendors hawking fresh meats, vegetables, and tropical staples on row upon row of vertical display stands.

The shopping list was always the same: bags of rice and beans, eggs, some bacalao to make codfish fritters or sautéed codfish with a side of yautia or ñame root vegetables, chicken parts, plantains for tostones or mofongo, and cornmeal for my favorite fried sorullitos.

Grandma would then treat me to a meat empanada or a piragua, a snow cone saturated with fruit syrup. It made the tedious trek back home and up the six flights absolutely worthwhile.

After picking us up from school and preparing dinner, Grandma would sit for hours into the night at her hand-driven sewing machine and make clothes for us. She taught me how to make dolls with old nylon stockings stuffed with scraps of material. Little buttons were sewn onto the head for eyes, and thick black thread was used to make a smiling mouth. The best part was taking leftover fabric and making tiny clothes for the doll.

Mother always tried to buy us special outfits for Easter, but our everyday attire was hand-me-down or handmade clothes that had to last until we either outgrew them or wore them to shreds. As I got older, I learned how to sew clothes without a pattern from Grandma and made my own outfits with fabrics of my choosing.

On the Saturdays when it was Wanda's turn to accompany Grandma to La Marqueta, I would stay home and help Mother clean the house. Music in the background was a must to keep up the spirits and maintain the momentum. Mother would stack the 78s onto the old Victrola and blast her favorites: Felipe Rodriguez, Daniel Santos, Trio Los Panchos. I knew the words to all the songs.

Out came the broom and the King Pine to mop the flowered shabby linoleum. Off came the cushions of the plastic-covered sofa bed to search for food crumbs or loose change in the crevices. Windows up to air out the house, flowered plastic curtains billowing in the wind.

Occasionally, she would end the housecleaning with a *sahumerio* or smudging—incense bought at the botanica spiritualist shop was burned on a metal pan and spread through the four corners of every room to ward off evil spirits and bring good fortune.

Grandma was a gifted herbalist and healer who could invent concoctions for every ailment you could think of. Family members and friends of friends would come to her for her herbal remedies and hands-on healing, and many would swear she had cured them of their maladies.

When we had colds, she would slap on our chests a warm, pink, pasty mixture and cover it with a cotton dressing. Then she would put *cebo de flande* or mutton tallow on the soles of our feet and lightly pass the flame of a candle over them. Pungent ginger tea or sweet chamomile tea calmed our upset stomachs.

Sometimes we would awaken in the middle of the night to find Grandma stuffing our noses or smearing our chests with the heavily mentholated Vicks Vaporub.

"Pero Mamá, what are you doing?"

"Stop fussing. It will help you breathe better," she'd say.

No Puerto Rican household would be complete without Alcolado Relampago, a commercially prepared alcohol rub made with natural herbal extracts, used to treat muscular aches and headache.

If anything made us kids run for the hills, it was Grandma coming at us with a tablespoon of cod liver oil, the most revolting, foul-smelling medicine known to mankind. She claimed it would make us strong and healthy, but I would've rather eaten a bowlful of raw squid than drink that stuff.

At night, it was the sound of Grandma's whispered prayers that calmed our fears and lulled us to sleep.

3

Mother Dearest

My mother was Mamá's second to youngest child, whom she named Ana. "She was a handful!" Grandma would say. "Always running around with the boys, hardheaded, and with such a fiery temper, ay Dios!" As a youngster, she was mischievous—as a teen-ager, rebellious.

At seventeen, she met a handsome soldier named Raul, and a clandestine courtship ensued. Just before Raul was shipped off to Korea, my mother discovered that she was pregnant. Not wanting to leave my mother in this scandalous predicament, Raul did the honorable deed and married her.

Six months later, she gave birth to a daughter she named Ada Nydia. But her joy would be short-lived when, at three months, Ada Nydia also succumbed to a fatal bout of dysentery.

It wasn't long before my mother became pregnant again. I was privileged to come into this world in a proper hospital room, and eleven months later, my sister Wanda was born.

By then, my father had returned from the war, but the separations, my mother's temper, and her mother-in-law's intrusions began to form a fractious wedge in their already fragile relationship. It was after Wanda's birth that my mother decided to move to New York.

Now in her mid-twenties, my mother was petite and well-proportioned, with flawless sun-kissed skin the color of peeled plantains. She wore her raven shoulder-length hair curled around the edges like a floral garland, which she accomplished by twisting strands of hair and flattening them in place with bobby pins overnight.

In the morning, she'd pick out the curls with the sharp end of a comb and lacquer them in place. She liked her skirts narrow and tight to just below the knees, her tiny feet in spiked heels, and her signature large hooped earrings on her delicate ears.

She always shaved her eyebrows and then carefully drew them in with an eyebrow pencil, creating a perfect curvilinear accent above her mischievous brown eyes. Fiery red lipstick was applied to her fleshy lips. The end result was strikingly beautiful indeed.

Mother had always been an outgoing person, and her life would not have been complete without cohorts to socialize with over a cup of café Bustelo or a game of loteria (bingo). That's how she met my biggest nemeses and worst nightmares.

Georgina, nicknamed Gina, lived on the fifth floor with her husband and three young daughters. This pint-sized despot with tiny curls ruled her home with an iron fist, and her tyranny was known to enmesh other people's children, namely us. The smallest offense was cause for criticism, an activity that usually called for a reflexive smack from Mother, to Gina's great delight, I was sure.

"Ana, look at what she's doing!" she'd point out to Mother. Off came Mother's slipper and WHOP! I hated Gina.

Then there was Conchita who lived on the third floor and was also friendly with the despot. She too was short with curly black hair and coffee-colored skin, complete with a large café-au-lait birthmark on her cheek. This Phantom of the Opera clone relished in criticism brimming with sarcasm.

"Young lady, you look like a Christmas tree with that dress. Where's the snow?" she'd say to me in Spanish.

What really infuriated me was when she acted supportive towards my mother, then bashed her behind her back in front of us. I hated her too.

Both gossipmongering *chismosas* got theirs when years later, Gina's husband declared enough and left her. Her three daughters eventually lost their way and ended on paths of self-destruction and enduring poverty, an aftermath I don't rejoice in as they were beautiful girls.

After Conchita's husband died, she hooked onto a younger man, whom her eldest daughter later seduced. In the end, they reaped what they sowed.

Mother was happiest when she had people around her, especially on festive occasions with lots of friends and family and lively music. She loved to dance and could shimmy in her tight skirts and stilettos until the wee hours of the morning.

It was my seventh birthday and Wanda's sixth when Mother decided to throw one of her famous fiestas. The tiny apartment was crammed with people having a good time, the laughter and chatter competing with the loud music.

By 11:00 p.m., I was tired and sleepy, but my uncle insisted on taking a picture of Wanda and me in front of the cake.

"But Tio, I don't want to take a picture now. I'm tired," I whined, squirming in front of the decorated table.

"Isabel, just hold still for one minute. Look at you. You look so pretty in your party dress," he coaxed.

"No, I don't want to!"

"Isabel, do as your uncle says. Stand still and let him take the picture," my mother commanded, anger seeping into her voice.

"No, Mother. I'm tired now. I don't want to!" I started to cry.

Mother swooped down on me like a goaded vulture, grabbed me by my long hair, and dragged me into the bedroom where she beat the daylights out of me, instructed me to remove my party dress, and sit in the room for the rest of the night.

"Don't you ever embarrass me like that in front of my guests," she breathlessly admonished me as I cowered in a corner sobbing.

When my brothers came along, Gilbert first then Edwin, Mother was merciless with them, especially Gilbert, who was sassy and had a clumsy tendency to break things. We were even more vulnerable when she returned home from work, tired and stressed.

Having to find creative ways to entertain ourselves in that tiny apartment, Wanda and I once made a makeshift swing from a bed sheet slung across the bedroom doorway.

"Edwin, Gilbert, come see what we made!"

"Oh, wow! Let me get on. I want to go first!" Gilbert shrieked. Edwin stood quietly nearby, a smile of amusement on his face, while Gilbert giggled incessantly as we swung him to and fro. We let them take turns, tickled by their screeching and laughter.

"Come, children!" shouted Grandma as she beckoned us to the kitchen for dinner.

Wanda and I rushed to the table and dug ravenously into Grandma's delicious rice and stewed beef, oblivious to our brothers' antics in our rudimentary playground.

Suddenly, we heard the crash of broken porcelain in the next room. We all ran to Mother's bedroom and saw Gilbert and Edwin frozen in front of the swing, staring at the shattered lamp on the floor.

"Oh, my god, who did that?" I asked, panicked. Gilbert and Edwin simultaneously pointed a finger at each other, but we all knew who the probable culprit was.

"Gilbert, Mother is going to be so angry when she gets home!" Gilbert started to cry, and Edwin began to whimper.

"Quick, let's clean this up and get rid of the swing." I put my arm around my inconsolable little brother, who instinctively knew that his hours were numbered. "Don't worry, Gilbert. We'll clean this up, and maybe she won't notice the lamp is gone. If you don't stop crying, she'll know something's wrong. Now go eat your dinner," I instructed him as I dried his tears with the hem of my dress.

When Mother came home from work that evening and found out, she grabbed Gilbert by the hair and began to beat his head against the wall, releasing her anger in an eruption of physical violence and profanity.

"*Sinverguenza*, what were you doing playing in my room! I paid good money for that lamp, you little bastard!"

Not being able to stand his tears, I stepped between them and got the brunt of her punches. It's something none of us likes to talk about anymore, but each one of us bears the marks of our mother's abuse in our own ways.

Mother would mention it almost with pride in her voice. "It's how I kept all of you in line."

To this day, though distance and personal obligations have separated us, we are very protective of each other whenever life's punches look our way through our mother's eyes.

Confined high up on the sixth floor of that moatless tower, we were never allowed to wander past the long hallway leading from our apartment door to the stairs. Everywhere we went, we had to hold tightly to Mother or Grandma's hand lest some bogeyman come along and snatch us. We were made to feel that the whole world was evil and everything outside our walls was to be feared.

The panic attacks began when I was eight years old. I couldn't cross the street unless someone dragged me along, often with my eyes closed. It felt as if I were crossing a planked rope bridge across an immense chasm.

On our weekly assembly days at school, my class had to march down a long aisle towards the front and center row of seats in a large auditorium. When the piano music began, signaling the beginning of the march, I would become paralyzed, unable to move, to talk, my stomach in a knot.

Eventually, my mother was called in to school, and I was referred to a psychologist for evaluation. I looked forward to seeing him because he'd have me play games with him and draw pictures and figure out what the weird black splotches represented. But after three sessions of testing, my mother decided that this was a lot of foolishness on my part and refused to take me back.

"What am I taking you there for? To draw pictures? I don't have time for that!" she'd complain.

As if that wasn't bad enough, I was brushing my long beautiful hair in front of the mirror one day, when I noticed a bald spot on the crown of my head. Before long, another bald spot appeared and then another, and soon I had several balding patches all over my scalp. I was devastated.

In an effort to cheer me up, Mother took me to Santita's Beauty Parlor to see if she could fix my hair so that the bald spots wouldn't be so obvious. Big mistake.

All the busybodies came rushing out from under their hair dryers to observe the sideshow oddity, offering remedies which my mother readily took onboard.

"Ana, this is very strange. You should take her to a spiritualist. Maybe there's an evil spirit inside her that needs to be cast out."

"*Mira*, rub some coconut oil on her scalp, and she will be cured in no time," another woman suggested.

For a week, I wore stinking coconut oil slathered on my scalp, but all I got was greasy hair.

Mother finally took me to the clinic where several baffled doctors probed my scalp like maternal chimps plucking insects off their young. They decided to try steroid shots to my scalp, which thankfully worked, and my hair eventually grew back.

4

Pernil and Pizza

E very year, the Italians held their Feast of Saint Anthony of Padua two blocks from my street, on East 108th Street. Tented stalls lined the street with delicious pastries, gelato, and mouthwatering meats and dishes cooked al fresco. Sparkly green, white, and red decorations stretched across the street, attached high up on lampposts, with streamers hanging down onto the confetti-strewn pavement.

Italian voices mixed with English could be heard straining over the music of Frank Sinatra, Connie Francis, and Jerry Vale, which blasted from huge speakers on either side of the street.

In the center of the block against an unobstructed building wall was a colossal statue of St. Anthony with donated dollar bills cascading down its garment.

It was the biggest party I'd ever seen, and we loved being a part of it, even though we didn't understand the language or the tradition.

The greatest time of all was Christmas, especially after other family members joined us on the mainland. Following the American tradition, we believed in "Santa Clos," and Mother kept the magic of not knowing alive.

On Christmas Eve, we would put rice in a bowl for the reindeer and then nestle together under the blankets and wait for sleep for, according to Mother, he would not come as long as we were awake. Gina and Conchita would keep her company and make sure we were all sleeping.

In the morning, there under the artificial tinseled tree would be presents galore, and though we never asked for anything, we knew it would be something we'd love. There were life-like dolls almost as tall as me, miniature tea sets and little dolls with tiny wardrobes, baby carriages and Colorforms Paste-Ons. They weren't extravagant or expensive, but to us, they were priceless.

The night before, Grandma would get busy making pasteles, a traditional dish made of rice or ground plantains stuffed with savory meat, while Mother prepared the roast pork. Early in the morning, the pork shoulder would go into the oven, the pasteles into the oversized cauldron for boiling, the rice with pigeon peas into a large pot for steaming.

All through the day, the aroma of roast pork would spread throughout the apartment and out into the hallway, enticing guests to come and enjoy the delicacies. For dessert, we would have flan, a delicious crème caramel custard with a hardy cup of Bustelo coffee.

The alcoholic beverage of choice was always a glass of Manischewitz wine, made popular by its size and inexpensive price tag. Guests were encouraged to bring their own liquor for neither Mother nor Grandma indulged in alcoholic drinks except for a taste on holidays.

Someone would inevitably bring a bottle of homemade coquito, a deceptively delectable holiday drink made with eggs, coconut milk, vanilla, cinnamon, and Bacardi rum. One glass of coquito was enough to make one feel blissfully inebriated; more than two was enough to make one shamefully fancy-free with a sorry case of amnesia and a thumping headache the next day.

At nightfall, the small apartment would be filled with friends and family who had followed us to America. The wicked stepsisters Gina and Conchita would be there, as well as other neighbors that my mother had befriended. Out came Mother's liveliest music, and somehow, they would all partner up in the tiny living room and dance the night away. Oh, what a wonderful time that was!

I didn't mind the trips to visit with Mother's old friends. A custom that had its roots back in the homeland, we could show up at any acquaintances' door unannounced and be cheerfully welcomed into their homes and they to ours. I would play with their kids while the women chatted for hours over cups of coffee and slices of buttered lard bread and wedges of Edam cheese.

If we stayed late enough, we would be treated to dinner, no matter how scarce their provisions were.

During the summer evening hours, Mother and some of our neighbors would take folding chairs downstairs and park themselves on the front stoop of our building. Soon, other tenants began doing the same. It was one of the few times my sister and I could enjoy the outdoors.

I can still hear the music blaring from the bodega next door and the Italian boys singing doo wop on the corner, and I can still see the girls dancing in front of the jukebox at Nancy's pizzeria.

Mother would sometimes take me to the Cosmo Theater on East 116th Street, where we'd watch Spanish flicks through a haze of cigarette smoke, the movie barely audible over the noise of people talking and kids crying and the crunch of candy wrappers.

I especially enjoyed the films with Cantinflas, the heart-warming clownish character made famous by Mario Moreno, Mexico's greatest comedic actor. It's there that I fell in love with Joselito, the Spanish child actor and singer, and Sandro, the Adonis-like Argentinean crooner and screen idol.

I loved accompanying her to the shows at Teatro Puerto Rico in the Bronx, where I was privileged to see live the singers she loved to listen to on her vinyl 78s.

Little did I know that those fleeting moments of happiness would become just that, for things were about to get complicated.

5

He Ain't Heavy

Mother had a few love interests through the years but had the sense not to allow any sleepovers, I suppose mainly out of respect for Grandma, who would've had a say about it. But this one was special.

He was a handsome police officer, and as an eight-year-old, I was at first more impressed by his uniform than by his polite manner and kind demeanor.

Mother would bring me along to meet him at whatever foot patrol post he'd been assigned to, and I'd stand there for hours while they chatted and got acquainted. I often wondered why she always met him in some clandestine spot until I came to the realization that he was already married.

A year or two later, my brother was born and was named Gilbert after him. Another two years passed, and then Edwin was born.

Occasionally, Gilberto senior would arrive drunk at the door after a late night with the boys, and he would end up sleeping over. I appreciated when he stayed over as Mother tended to be less attentive towards us, and we could wreak havoc without fear of being punished.

Gilberto became the father figure Wanda and I never had. He'd always show up unexpectedly every so often and announce, "Get dressed kids. We're going out." The resounding response would be deafening.

It didn't matter where he was taking us for we knew it would be someplace different and fun. Sometimes it would be City Island to eat seafood or to the park for a fun day out. He'd take us to Palisades Amusement Park where we'd jump on all the colorful fun rides and eat cotton candy and shoot the clown in the mouth with a water pistol until the balloon above his head burst. He became a part of our extended family and would join us for family outings to the beach or the ball park.

When little Gilbert arrived, his father would come by more frequently and helped financially with his needs. But by the time Edwin arrived, Gilberto began to lose his patience with my mother, who was so easily driven to fits of rage. Eventually, he stopped coming around altogether.

I was eight years old when my oldest brother was born. I took care of him like he was my baby doll, changing his diapers, feeding and dressing him. I still make him laugh when I tell him about the times he baptized me with squirts of pee.

Little Gilbert, or Kino as we eventually nicknamed him, was the active one, always getting into some mischief out of curiosity or boredom.

In preparation for dinner one evening, Grandma had placed a pot of water on the stove. Curious to see what was cooking, he tilted the pot towards him and spilled the hot water over the side of his face and neck.

He suffered third degree burns which turned into blisters, then scabs which had to be surgically removed over a period of time. I accompanied Mother to all his clinic visits and held his little hand while he screamed as the scabs were debrided. It was horrible!

He also had a very short fuse. At suppertime one day, he got angry with me and came towards me like a matador, fork in hand, and impaled my kneecap. He got a sound whipping for that.

Edwin, on the other hand, was a pale, sickly child who developed asthma attacks early on and bouts of enteritis. During one of his hospitalizations for dehydration, Conchita and Gina came to visit. As Mother walked away, Conchita could be heard saying, "That's what happens when you feed your kid junk food." I could've kicked her.

Edwin was also quiet and shy and prone to doing strange things. We had a cat aptly called Kitty, and one day, we couldn't find her.

We looked everywhere for Kitty. "Misoo, misoo," we called out to her, under the beds, in the closets, beneath the sofa.

As Grandma began to prepare for dinner, she opened the refrigerator, and there was poor Kitty shivering next to the butter. We figured out instantly who the culprit was. One day, Kitty disappeared entirely, and although we guessed who might have been responsible, we never questioned her whereabouts and never got another cat.

We were raised in the Catholic faith but were not devout Catholics, attending church only on special holidays. The inside of a church has always been so solemn and sacred to me. We were always taught to respect it and the people who dedicated their lives to it.

When I was ten years old and Wanda nine, my mother enrolled us in catechism class to prepare for our first communion.

Father Louis was a stocky, pint-sized, balding priest with bad teeth and putrid breath, who ran the classes like a commanding officer, ruler in hand. He was to be feared.

Every session, he would choose a child to stand next to him in front of the class and read from the catechism book. Inevitably, it became my turn.

He sat in his chair behind his desk and called me to the front. As I read, he pulled me gently towards him and placed his hand on the back of my thighs. The following week, he did the same thing, but this time, he was kneading my thighs.

I thought this was very odd and felt very uncomfortable, but I dared not say anything for fear of being reprimanded. Who would believe me?

The next class, he called me up to the front again. I was so scared and apprehensive, I started to get nauseous. I didn't like this old, ugly, disgusting man touching me.

As I began to read, I felt his hand on my leg, slowly rising, inching its way up my dress. The nausea started to envelope me. His hand finally reached my crotch and he started to squeeze. I threw up all over his desk.

In our early teens, Wanda and I still weren't allowed to leave the apartment without a chaperone. Since we couldn't afford to buy records or magazines, we relied heavily on the radio and our tiny television set to provide us with entertainment and a window to the outside world. Though we were raised listening to Spanish music, we soon developed a passion for American rock 'n roll.

After school, Wanda and I would run up the six flights of stairs, ahead of Grandma, to watch Shindig and Hullabaloo. We'd turn on the radio and write down and memorize the lyrics to all of our favorite songs. And then came the greatest phenomenon to hit the airwaves—the Beatles came to America and conquered our hearts. The British invasion soon followed, and we became wholly embroiled in the music and the fanaticism.

In my daydreams, I fantasized about the faraway land they came from—what it would be like to be in Liverpool. I would listen to Gerry and the Pacemakers and, in my vivid imagination, be on that ferry crossing his beloved Mersey and feel the wind in my hair and see the landscape on either side of the river. I could stand on Penny Lane and see the barber showing photographs and watch Eleanor Rigby leaving a jar by the church door. The music brought consummate joy and meaning to our lives.

Thus began a dichotomous introduction to a bicultural world of Spanish music and rock 'n roll, rice and beans and peanut butter and jelly sandwiches, Spanish novels with cartoon drawings and Archie and Veronica comics, Three Kings' Day and Santa Claus, spoken Spanish at home and

English in school. We embraced the assimilation into the mainstream culture while maintaining our rich traditions at home. And we were that much better off for it.

6

King King on the Fire Escape

It was in the early sixties that my Uncle Anibal, his beautiful wife Josefina, and son Louie moved into the apartment across from us. Our front doors were no more than four feet apart.

Louie, who was my same age, became my best friend and partner in mischief. We spent every possible moment of our days together and shared the same love of music. His father liked to buy all the latest records, and Louie, Wanda, and I would spend hours at his place, listening to music, miming the words, and choreographing dance steps, pretending to be members of the group.

Uncle Anibal was an alcoholic. When he was sober, he was meek and mild-mannered. But whenever he got drunk, he would become an angry beast, and for some unknown reason, he'd come after my mother, banging on our door and calling her ugly names.

I used to get really scared when that happened because his rage was so intense, I knew he'd hurt my mother if he got his hands on her.

Once, Uncle Anibal came pounding on our door, shamelessly drunk.

"Ana, open the door, you slut!" he yelled in Spanish. I wondered if I should hide or run...but where?

"Come through here," Mother called to us as she opened the fire escape gate and sneaked out the window.

"Oh no, I'm not going out there! We're so high up!" I whined. But it was either climb up the fire escape stairs to the roof or risk getting pummeled by King Kong.

"Wait for me, Mother!" I yelled as I climbed out the window behind Wanda and Mother. Survival instinct pushed me to make it to the roof without looking down.

We stayed there until the banging stopped, then we carefully tiptoed down the hallway stairs from the roof, making sure that my deranged uncle wasn't still standing at the door.

Luckily he was gone. We ran into the apartment and securely locked the deadbolt, the two locks, and the chain on the door.

Every now and then, Conchita or Gina would ask Mother, "Are they señoritas yet?" referring to Wanda and me. I had no clue what they were going on about, so I asked my school buddy, Maria, what they meant.

"That's when you get your 'friend.'" She went on to explain, like it was the darkest secret in the world. "Every month, you start bleeding through there."

"Through where?" I asked.

"You know, through there, your chochita, where you pee from," she whispered.

"Nooooo!"

"Yep, and if you kiss a boy while you have your friend, you can get pregnant," she added.

"Nooooo!"

I made a mental note of that and underlined it. Wanda got it first but never said anything. As time went on, we just understood that it had happened but was not something up for discussion, nor did we ever feel comfortable sharing such a secret with Mother or Grandma. I suppose Mother figured it out when her sanitary pads started to disappear.

Debbie Wright was a porcelain-skinned, freckle-faced, free-spirited girl who lived on the ground floor of our building with her grandmother and mother, both of whom smoked like chimneys. Debbie became my good friend and often climbed the six flights to play with me since I was not allowed to leave the apartment without my mother.

I was fourteen years old and soon developed a crush on Debbie's cousin, Jesse—a tall handsome rebel with smooth jet-black hair and dreamy brown eyes. At the same time, my cousin Louie had a liking for Debbie, while another friend named Chachi had expressed a keen interest in Debbie's brother, Tony.

One glorious Christmas, during a holiday feast at my house, all six of us crammed into Mother's tiny bedroom, unbeknown to the party revelers, who were having a rowdy good time in the next room.

The boys lined up against the wall behind the closed door while the girls stood facing them, each couple engaged in small talk.

Jesse and I were completely focused on each other, and at one point, he gently took hold of my hands as we chatted about school and friends and music.

As time went by, the world around Jesse and me began to fade away until it was just the two of us. My swelling pubescent hormones set a thousand butterflies free in my belly, and my heart beat with such intensity, its thumping seemed to rise above the din of music and laughter.

An awkward moment of silence gelled into a tender, loving gaze. His handsome face began to come towards me in slow motion.

Oh no...is he going to kiss me? What am I supposed to do here?

I thought of the Spanish soap operas that we all gathered to watch every night and pictured the handsome lead actor with his swooning lover in his arms. Let's see...eyes close, head tilts, lips part and come together...then what?

I watched as his perfect lips came closer, slowly separated, then gently touched mine, and as the heavens opened up, his tongue thrust into my mouth and hit clenched teeth. We each drew back suddenly with a surprised look, but not for the same reasons.

"What's the matter? Don't you wanna kiss?" he asked.

I was confused. What was the tongue action all about?

"Nnnoo, it's not that. I'm...I'm just a little nervous, that's all."

It suddenly occurred to me that if we kissed, I could get pregnant, but Maria said that it would only happen if I had my "friend" and I didn't, so I guessed it would be all right.

Jesse held me close for a timeless moment, then he lifted my face up to his and repeated the gesture while I resolved to give in and return his motions in kind.

It all became so natural then, this slow melding of smell and breath and taste, like the first succulent tang of a ripe mango, the way it leaves one yearning for one more and another, until satiety ends the hunger but not the lingering taste.

Afterwards, I wondered if this meant we were now boyfriend and girlfriend and what that involved. I would never get the chance to find out.

Jesse and I never got the opportunity to be alone again as Mother's rules prohibited him from visiting me.

Eventually, he moved away and stopped coming around. I was heartbroken.

7

Return to Paradise

Grandma's eldest son, Enrique, was an army drill sergeant who served in Korea with the 65th Infantry Regiment. Nicknamed "The Borinqueneers," it was a segregated unit consisting primarily of Puerto Rican soldiers from the island who, in 2016, were awarded the Medal of Honor. Sadly, Uncle Enrique never got to experience the honorary recognition.

He returned to his birthplace, San Germán, after retiring from the armed forces. A bald-headed, stocky, gruff-voiced bulldog, he spoke in loud commands, even when it was just casual conversation. "That chicken was delicious!" he'd yell to the person sitting next to him at the dinner table.

I was in my early teens when I came home from school one day, and Grandma announced, "I'm going to Puerto Rico to visit Enrique and Ana Isabel in June, and we decided that you can come with me."

"What? You mean it?"

"Sí, Isabel. Your mother doesn't want me to fly alone, and since Enrique is buying my ticket, we're going to put some money together so you can come too."

I crossed off the days on my calendar, saved my pennies, and began to gather essential items weeks before our departure. Having no recollection of Puerto Rico, it would be like seeing the island for the first time. I couldn't wait.

We packed enough clothes for three weeks into two old and battered suitcases, and with my cheap Japanese camera in hand, Grandma and I boarded a Pan American flight headed to San Juan.

The plane ride was scary with all those people stuffed like sardines in a claustrophobic oblong space that shook and took cyclone dips whenever it hit an air pocket. By the time we landed, my inner organs felt like they had exchanged places—my heart pounding in my belly, my intestines stuck in my throat.

We walked through tunnel-like passages, and as we emerged into the blinding sunlight, the pageantry that opened up before me was unlike anything I could ever imagine.

A trio of guitarists played a welcoming *aguinaldo* while men in guayabera shirts and Panama hats and women in pastel dresses warmly embraced their loved ones. The sun shone like a brilliant spotlight as the palm trees swayed lazily to the whispers of a sultry breeze. It was as if a vibrant watercolor mural had come to life.

Cab drivers with enviable tans swarmed arrivals, offering rides in Spanish to any city on the island.

Since we were not expecting Tio Enrique to pick us up, we boarded a rickety cab for the four-hour ride to San Germán. According to my map, we would be crossing La Cordillera Central, a vast mountain range that extends from the center of the island to the southwest.

Beyond the outskirts of Isla Verde, we rode down dirt country roads, past farmlands and sugar cane fields, overtaking farmers on horseback pulling carts full of hay and freshly picked crops.

At some point, the car began its ascent into the mountains, where the road became curvy and narrower. Modest cement and wooden houses dotted the roadway, some painted in striking Crayola colors and flanked by graceful flamboyán trees.

We passed shack-like bodegas with music blaring from wide open doors, vendors selling quenepas or Spanish limes and mangoes on wooden carts, and mouth-watering spit-roasted pork being sold on the roadsides.

Up, up, up sputtered the old clunker into the mountains, around heart-stopping hairpin bends, honking at every turn to warn obscured oncoming traffic that we were in their path.

As the brush cleared along my side of the road, I yelped as I realized how close we were to the edge of the precipice. When I dared to look, I could see tiny little houses precariously perched on the sides of the valley below and wondered what stopped them from rolling down the mountain.

We finally made it down the foothills none too soon and arrived at Tio Enrique's house as the sun began to set. He and his wife rushed out to greet us, and as he bear-hugged Grandma, I could see tears in his eyes.

They immediately sat us at the dinner table where his wife, Ana Isabel, laid out a sumptuous feast for us to enjoy. The conversation through dinner was animated and loud, with Tio Enrique barking out questions like volleys of cannon blasts. I'm sure the neighbors knew we had arrived.

Just before bedtime, he put his burly arm around me and ordered me to have a good time and make myself at home.

During the next few weeks, while my uncle was at work, Ana Isabel took us sightseeing and to the beach. I had never seen the splendor of such azure-green ocean water as it washed up and dropped off crabs and beautiful pink seashells and conches onto the pristine sandy blanket.

Grandma told me to pick up a conch and listen, and I was amazed to hear the hollow sound of the ocean's roar. I took the conch with me, after Grandma inspected it for inhabitants, and carefully packed it in my bag so that my brothers and sister back home could hear the ocean too.

At night, we'd sit out on the porch sipping on a refreshing glass of mabi while listening to the singing of the coqui, a small frog endemic to Puerto Rico. I especially loved to sit on the balcony when it rained and watch the drops pelt the large leaves of the banana plants and smell the freshness of wet soil.

Ana Isabel took Grandma and me to visit Grandma's eldest daughter, Zaida, whom I had never met. Zaida lived on the outskirts of San Germán, past miles of dirt roads and hilly countryside.

We came upon a very poor area with wooden shacks on stilts and barefoot children playing in mud puddles. Leaving the car behind, we walked up a rocky, perilously inclined hill until we reached a plateau where more wooden houses were situated.

In the time it took us to climb the mini Mt. Everest, someone must have told Zaida that she had visitors for she appeared at the top of the hill, running towards us barefoot and with arms outstretched. Oddly enough, Grandma and Zaida rarely kept in touch, but now they were greeting and embracing one another as though the long silence had not fractured their bond.

Zaida took us to her modest home and cheerfully welcomed us inside, where she got busy making a pot of coffee using a colander made out of fabric as a filter.

The two-room shack had a wood-burning stove in a corner with the kitchen sink just outside a rear window. The tiny living area was sparsely decorated with a table and a few scruffy chairs. Faded photos of Jesus and Virgin Mary were conspicuously tacked to a wall.

There was something about the simplicity and humility of her home that I found cozy and comforting, like a child's old, tattered blanket.

Suddenly, the skies turned an ominous gray as a few raindrops began to fall and create musical tones on the rusty tin roof—tick, tick, plop, tick. As the women caught up on lost years, I quietly fell asleep on a frayed armchair.

The three weeks went by very quickly, but I brought home memories and wonderful pictures that captured special moments forever.

8

El Gran Combo and the Revolution

We finally managed to move out of the railroad flat and into a two-bedroom, roach-infested hole in upper Manhattan on 124th Street. It was dark and dreary, with a long, windowless entry hallway leading to a galley kitchen on the right. A little further down was the living room, which opened onto a bedroom, partitioned off with flowered curtains.

We brought with us the plastic covered sofa and armchairs, the chipped stand-up TV console, and the stained Victrola, all of which fit nicely into our small living area.

To the left of the main bedroom was a smaller one where Mother placed bunk beds for Wanda, Gilbert, and Edwin. Grandma slept on a cot next to the bunk beds, and I slept with Mother in the larger bedroom.

The best features of our new home was that the bathtub was in the bathroom, a closet-like space in the kitchen. It had the extra bedroom, and it was only three flights up instead of six. But once again, the windows faced the backyard, where lofty tenements obstructed the morning rays of the sun.

Cousin Louie and his parents had stayed behind at their apartment on 106th Street, and I missed him terribly. A year later, Maria and I graduated from middle school and went our separate ways. Conchita and Gina eventually moved to the Bronx and, unfortunately, it would not be the last I'd see of that pair.

By now, Mother had stopped working after an injury to her wrist, and once her worker's compensation ran out, she went on public assistance. I understood that she had little choice but felt humiliated by it just the same as I knew that the kids at school would make fun of Wanda and me if they ever found out.

Even worse, she was home all the time now and able to keep a closer eye on us. We really had to be on our Ps and Qs for, although we were getting older, we would not be spared the wrath of Mother, whose lightning quick whacks and vulgar tongue-lashings continued to be dished out for the slightest offense.

The one redeeming factor was that we were now allowed to visit the public library, which was one block away from our building. Books once again became an immersive refuge from the squalor and indignities of my own reality, each page offering a portal into lives and experiences that fed my fantasies and enriched my existence.

My vivid imagination transported me to the beauty of Thoreau's *Walden Pond*, to the streets of China in Pearl Buck's *The Good Earth*, to nineteenth century England in Dickens' *David Copperfield*, to a floating hospital in *A Ship Called Hope*. But my absolute favorites were the Nancy Drew mysteries, and I read every single one.

I decided to attend Benjamin Franklin High School on 116th Street in Manhattan since Mother insisted that the school be within walking distance of our neighborhood. I was a bit apprehensive about this big change as, not only did I not know anyone there, but I was also getting ready to join an older crowd.

The year was 1967. Hippies, bell bottoms, and love beads, acid rock and outdoor music festivals made their appearance. The Vietnam War sparked conscientious objectors and protests. Riots erupted in the inner cities as dejected poor people sought an outlet for their frustrations.

For my sister and me, adapting to these extrinsic radical changes was a gradual process. Our own growing pains took precedence over understanding what was going on at the time, compelling and in-your-face as it was. But we were young and naïve, and it was that innocence and instinctive need to escape the stark reality of our home that made us gravitate towards the peaceful side of this sweeping social revolution.

Although the high school that I, and later Wanda, attended consisted primarily of Black and Hispanic students, our inability to socialize outside school hours prevented us from enjoying the same music and trends that the other kids

followed. We still enjoyed listening to Spanish music whenever Mother played her 78s, but they were mostly old school
songs with a Gran Combo LP thrown in every now and
then. Mostly we listened to Cousin Bruce and Wolfman Jack
on the radio and watched mainstream American shows on
TV.

Music was everything to us. We graduated from the
teeny-bopper tunes of Herman's Hermits, Paul Revere and
the Raiders, and the Young Rascals to the harsh acid rock of
Jimi Hendrix, Cream, and Vanilla Fudge.

But my biggest idol was Janis Joplin. Her every song and
emotional nuance touched my soul deeply because she sang
and cried out about me. I identified with her, became her. I
wore my long hair frizzy and unruly. Wide elephant pants
with velvet or tie-dyed shirts, bangles up to my elbows and
rows of hanging necklaces became my signature attire.

I associated with a handful of friends who enjoyed the
same music, and though my appearance was bizarre by other
students' standards, the other kids pretty much left me
alone, and that suited me just fine.

I first laid eyes on Alex in my freshman year of high
school. Tall and handsome with big, expressive brown eyes,
he was a real heartthrob. Alex was the drummer for a rock 'n
roll band and was extremely popular with the girls. I would
follow him around school, deliberately bumping into him,
hoping that he would take notice. One day, he did and struck
up a conversation, not surprisingly, about my hair and ban-

gles. We discovered that we had a lot in common, and he asked me if we could meet after school for a chat and a soda.

"Sure!" I said, trying very hard to contain my excitement. At sixteen, I was still not allowed to socialize with boys.

For the rest of the day, I vacillated between the thrilling possibility of spending time with Alex and the excuse I could give Mother for coming home late. Anything I said to her would be unacceptable, and I couldn't run the risk of having her come and look for me.

"I'm really sorry, Alex, but I have a pile of homework to do. I can't stay after school today."

"How about tomorrow or maybe Saturday afternoon? We could hang out in Central Park for a while."

"Alex, I'm not sure right now. Saturday is when I go food shopping with Mom, so I'll have to let you know, okay?"

I knew damn well this wasn't going to pan out, but stalling for time was better than telling him the truth. He looked disappointed, and as he walked away, I hoped he hadn't taken my excuses as a rejection.

We bumped into each other often at school, and though I had to persist with my lame stories, he made it clear that the invitation was always open.

Every day, I would go home and inscribe on the blank pages of my diary the flowery details of my encounters with Alex. I'd nestle under the blanket, and in the darkness, I would imagine us dancing, gazing into each other's eyes, holding hands.

Opportunity came knocking one day, but with a sticky twist. Mother had been hospitalized for an elective surgery, which left Grandma in charge. Grandma was not exactly a pushover, but she'd be more accepting of any reasonable excuse I gave her. I told her that I was going to visit Mother at the hospital after school, and she gave me permission to go.

I waited for Alex after school, and he courteously offered to walk with me to the hospital, which was seventeen gloriously long blocks away. We held hands as we chatted about school and friends and music. All the while, I glanced around to make sure that no one I knew, namely Conchita or Gina, saw me holding hands with him.

Once we got to my destination, it was clear that neither one of us wanted the conversation to end. He parked his backside against a lamppost and leaned me against him, my heart beating in synch with his, his breath blending with mine. I prayed that Mother's windows did not face the front entrance.

That thought quickly dissipated as it became evident that he was going to kiss me. He puckered his lips into a perfect O, came at me slowly, and like a sucker fish, attached his lips to mine and gave me the sloppiest wet kiss. When it was over, I could feel sticky saliva all over my mouth, my cheeks, and my chin. It was kind of gross, but I let him kiss me until I felt like I was drowning in drool.

I gently pushed him away and declared it was time to go see my mother, whose windows thankfully faced the back of the hospital. I had plenty to say to my diary that night.

We continued to see each other at school and hold hands and talk. I assumed that we were now boyfriend and girlfriend, though we never got the chance to kiss again, which, quite honestly, was a relief.

The school announced its annual talent show, and I knew that Alex had signed up to play with his band. I thought I'd better come up with a good excuse to give Mother because this was an event I just couldn't miss.

Being a member of the school choir, I told her that I needed to be there or I'd get a failing grade. She believed me. Not especially interested in hearing a bunch of school kids sing, Mother allowed me to go without her.

"You'd better be back by seven o'clock," I heard her say as I closed the door behind me.

I sat in an aisle seat and excitedly waited for Alex to make his grand entrance. I waited and waited. Finally, I turned around to see if he was standing around looking for me. There was Alex, sitting three rows behind me, smearing his saliva all over a girl who was immodestly perched on his lap.

I couldn't believe what I was seeing! I went up to them and just stared until they both came up for air and realized I was standing there.

"What is this?" I asked him indignantly, like I didn't know. I could feel the tears start to sting, but I wasn't going to cry in front of them.

"Nothing. She's just a friend of mine," he said, somewhat annoyed. The bimbo said nothing and didn't move. "Isabel, go sit down. I'll be there in a minute," he said.

Numb, like a zombie, I sat back down to wait for him. The show had already started, but I didn't see or hear any of it. I just sat there and stared straight ahead, fighting to keep from crying and wondering what I should do.

After a few minutes, I looked back, and Alex and his "friend" were gone. I picked myself up, and in a trance, walked out of there and went straight home. It wasn't until everyone was tucked in for the night and the lights went out that I allowed myself to quietly feel the pain of Alex's betrayal.

Back at school the following week, Alex pretended like nothing had happened, and I pretended like nothing was bothering me. I wasn't going to give him the satisfaction of knowing that he had broken my heart.

A few days later, I arrived home from school to find Mother waiting for me at the door, hand on hip, with a fierce look on her face. I could sense that dreadful sinking feeling one gets when you know you're going to get whacked but don't know why.

"What ees dis?" she wanted to know as she held up my diary.

I was stunned. How much did she read? How much did she understand?

"Who you kissing, so *cabrona*?"

"Mother, give me that!" I demanded, reaching for my diary.

"No, dis I read," she stated defiantly as she ran to the bathroom and locked herself in, my most intimate secrets in her hand.

I was screaming and banging on the door, tears flowing in desperation as I pleaded with her to give me back my book. Minutes later, the door opened, and without warning, she slapped me across the face with my diary and kept hitting me until she got tired, her breath coming in spasms.

"I never want to hear you are kissing wid dis Alex," she yelled, as I took what was left of my dignity and cowered to the back bedroom. In the end, he wasn't even worth it.

That summer, I lost a lot of weight and Mother started to allow me to wear light makeup. I showed up the next school year looking fabulous, and when Alex saw me, he came at me literally salivating like a rabid dog.

"Good Lord, you look terrific, girl! Are you going to be busy later?"

"Yes I am, but not with you. Good-bye, Alex." I never gave him the time of day after that.

All those trips to the hospital clinics as translator- in-residence for Mother and her friends had instilled in me a keen interest in the field of medicine, doubly inspired by Grandma's extraordinary healing abilities. It was she who fostered and supported what would become my ultimate goal in life.

Mother finally allowed me to leave the house unaccompanied when I expressed an interest in becoming a candy striper at Metropolitan Hospital a few blocks away. I looked forward to the weekends when I proudly put on my white and blue pin-striped uniform and reported for duty in the pediatric ward.

There, I would write down diagnoses and medications which I would later research in the treasured medical reference book that Grandma had gifted me that Christmas.

I got my first paying job when I was fifteen years old. Mother's friend Clarita and her husband owned a sweatshop on East 126th Street. During the summer months, I worked there a few days a week doing odd jobs: snipping threads off garments, preparing finished clothing for shipping, sweeping the floors at day's end.

I gave part of my wages to Mother, and I used the rest to buy vintage hippie clothes in secondhand shops, love beads, and teen magazines. When we didn't have enough money, Wanda and I would walk home from school instead of taking the bus, and we'd use the money to buy records.

On a bright and sunny Sunday morning, Wanda and I decided to hang out in Greenwich Village and experience being a part of the flower child scene. I was sixteen years old, and we had never been beyond the boundaries of El Barrio on our own. But we were ready to test the waters and take our chances, for we also had to lie to Mother about where we were going.

I came up with the brilliant excuse that I was taking Wanda to my volunteer job at the hospital so that she could see what I did there. Mother fell for the story, but she warned us to be home by five o'clock or else.

"Si, Mami, si, we'll be home by then," we promised.

We got on the train feeling very grown up and excited about being on our own and doing as we pleased.

Emerging from the darkness of the subway tunnel, we came upon a scene full of vibrancy, color, and music. There were lots of small shops selling peace signs and tie-dyed clothing and psychedelic posters, the strong scent of incense flowing from every doorway.

We found our way to Washington Square Park, where girls in peasant dresses and flowers in their hair danced with abandon to the rhythmic beat of conga drums. Guys with long, unkempt hair strummed guitars and sang folk songs off-key. Young people played with Frisbees in the grass with furry pets joining the fun, while a juggler in a clown outfit struggled with flying pins. It was a wonderful, peaceful, fun-loving "happening."

The hours passed too quickly, and we decided it was time go home. But where exactly did we end up, and where was the subway station?

We walked for several blocks looking for a train stop until we finally came to one that said "Uptown." We headed there since that was the direction we needed to go.

Wanda and I each had one token and a little loose change in our pockets. We jumped on the first train that came, but it wasn't long before we realized that we weren't familiar with any of the stops we had just passed. Where were we?

We decided to get off at the next stop, and figure this out. The tiled letters on the subway wall read 103rd Street, but this wasn't El Barrio! The platform was deserted now, without a soul in sight to ask for directions. Panic set in. We ran upstairs, and what a relief. There was a man in the booth just past the turnstile.

"Mister, can you please tell us how to get to 125th Street and Lexington?"

"Well, girls," said the nice man, "you're on the west side of town. You'll have to come out, go upstairs and cross the street to the other platform, take the train back downtown to 42nd Street, shuttle over to the east side, then take the uptown train again to 125th Street."

Wanda and I looked at each other like this gentleman had just given us instructions in Greek. Somewhat clueless, we followed his directions up until the part where we cross to the other side, and then forgot what the rest was. Even worse, we came to the dreadful realization that we had no tokens and didn't have enough money to buy two more.

Sheer panic gave way to frantic fear for our lives as we quickly became aware of the grueling punishment that awaited us if we didn't get home soon. We had no choice but to walk the rest of the way home.

Turning east, we decided to take a shortcut through Central Park as the skies began to turn a somber dusky gray. Finally, the 110th Street park exit was in sight, but so was the group of sinister female thugs swaggering towards us.

"Hey!" the frontline bully yelled at us. "I heard you wanted to beat us up!"

"W-w-why would we w-w-want to do that? W-w-we don't even know you."

Crap! How do we get out of this one?

"You got any money?" asked the grim reaper, as she and her lackeys emptied our pockets.

Oh boy, this is not going to be pretty, I thought.

"You ain't got no money, bitch?" yelled Medusa, with spit flying and fire in her eyes.

"No, and we don't want any trouble either so just leave us alone." Big mistake, or was it? Something told me anything I said would not get us out of this snake pit.

Suddenly, one of the girls snatched my love beads, and as the colorful stones rolled off the broken string, she began to pummel me with her fists, the rest of the evil mob joining in. My sister and I were both knocked to the pavement, my left knee hitting the concrete with a painful thud as they viciously kicked and punched, each blow sending a sharp ripple of pain through my ribs, my belly, my face.

I had lost sight of Wanda and was desperately trying to get away from the pack, when I heard her screaming, "Isabel, help me!" Two girls were dragging my sister towards the lake.

Like an enraged Goliath, I forcefully broke free and ran to her, pulling the punks off by their hair, digging my nails and teeth into arms and hands as the others continued to punch and kick me.

From somewhere in the distance, I heard the angry yell of a masculine voice. "What the hell are you doing? Get the fuck off them now!"

Everything stopped, and as we looked up, there was a man standing with what looked like a gun in his hand. The bruisers scampered off like mice scurrying for cover.

I held my sister as we both cried for what could have been, grateful for the presence of the angel that was sent to save us. The Good Samaritan helped us up and asked if we were okay and did we need to go to a hospital.

"No, we just need to get home. But thank you so much...thank you."

A young boy appeared on the scene, and in his hand was my brown paper bag with my uniform still in it. "Here, I think this is yours. I saw them throw it in the bushes," he said.

My sister and I slowly walked the rest of the way home in silence. There was no point in hurrying. Nothing needed to be said. We knew exactly what awaited us.

It was nightfall by the time we got to our building. Wanda apprehensively knocked on the door, and a neighbor opened it, my mother behind her.

"Where the hell have you been!" Mother shouted, as she shoved the neighbor aside.

She reached out and grabbed my sister's hair, pulling her while screaming hysterically, the neighbor trying to release Mother's grip from Wanda's locks. My sister somehow managed to escape past her.

Mother grabbed me and began to wildly punch and smack me.

"Where the hell have you been!" she screamed over and over until she succumbed to one of her infamous nerve attacks and landed on the floor, writhing and screeching uncontrollably.

It took a while for the neighbor and Grandma to calm her down, but by then, Wanda and I had found refuge in the small bedroom where we cried and cried until there were no more tears.

It would be a long time before Mother let us go out again without a chaperone.

Soon after we moved into the roach motel on 124th Street, my mother befriended two brothers who lived next door to us, and she started spending a lot of time in their apartment. I was old enough to know this was dubious, un-ladylike behavior, and it was humiliating to think she might be bumping uglies with one of these two oddballs.

Grandma apparently wasn't too happy either for, one night, she knocked on their door and unceremoniously pulled my mother out by her hair. It was the first and only time I ever saw Grandma get that angry.

The brothers were both in their mid-twenties. The youngest, Angel, was homely and not bad looking, but the eldest, Cayo, was so ugly, I felt sorry for him. He had tiny yellow buck teeth encrusted with plaque inside a pock-marked face. Tall and skinny with greasy curly hair, he gave the appearance of a Tsantsa shrunken head atop a bamboo spear.

Angel approached me one day and privately revealed that his brother, the aboriginal talking head, was secretly in love with me and wanted to know if I'd be his girl. I don't know what hypnotic rite the lovelorn relic had performed prior to asking, but I found myself saying yes.

The relationship only lasted five minutes.

Angel exchanged places with Cayo, and soon as I saw his zit-filled face floating towards me, I knew I couldn't go through with it, no matter how sorry I felt for him.

"I'm sorry, but my mother would never allow me to have a boyfriend. I have to say no."

"But she doesn't have to know. C'mon, say yes," he begged.

"If my mother ever found out, she would hurt us both. It won't work. Let's just stay friends."

"But I really like you. You're breaking my heart. How 'bout we give it a try?"

"No, I'm sorry. I have to insist now. Leave it alone. I'm not going to repeat myself." He shucked under his breath and walked away.

Months later, as Wanda, Mother, and I were casually walking down the street, my sister turned to me and said, "Isabel, mom has something to tell you."

I couldn't imagine what she had to say. After playing at twenty questions, pumping my sister and Mother for answers, Wanda nonchalantly announced, "She's going to have a baby."

My mouth fell open, my face burning with anger and embarrassment. "Whose baby is it?" I asked, thinking it probably belonged to one of the brothers next door.

"Mariano's," she said.

I was shocked. Mariano was a friend of the brothers and the least likely person that I thought mother would get involved with. He was also very married. It took me a long time to come to terms with this calamity.

My little sister was born on the fifth of July as the Independence Day celebrations wound down. The festive holiday fireworks were a befitting welcome for a child who would become the light of our lives. I named her Bernadette after the little peasant girl from Lourdes and the famous Four Tops song, one of my favorites.

Once again, I switched on my maternal role and spent most of my earnings from Clarita's sweatshop on buying little Bernie cute outfits and baby toys. It was worth it just to see her toothless smile light up her adorable pudgy face.

At some point after Bernadette's birth, Mother began to slacken the leash a little and allowed Wanda and me to go out, but always with strict regulations attached. We had to be home by a certain time, travel only certain distances or with an adult if outside the boundaries of El Barrio.

On the radio, Cousin Brucie announced that the Young Rascals, one of our favorite sixties groups, would be meeting fans near the bandshell at Central Park. My sister and I celebrated our independence by boldly skipping school that day and heading out to the park where we, along with a mob of other kids, started searching for Rascals around the main lawn like wild children scouting for Easter eggs.

"There they are!" someone shouted, and as we looked in the distance, I could see four little heads rising from the other side of the hill, the sun behind them creating a giant golden halo.

Like raging bulls, we all rushed towards them, Wanda and I tackling whoever was blocking our way to the field goal. I had my Japanese camera in hand, and as we reached them, Wanda grabbed her favorite, Eddie Brigati, by his signature neck kerchief, pulled him towards her, and planted a wet one on his cheek while I clicked away.

We never got to develop that film, but my sister got her wish and had a wonderful memory she'd talk about for years to come.

While in my junior year in high school, my sister and I got involved with a group of students who met after school to write and act out plays from improvisations based on real-life experiences. Maryat Lee, an award-winning playwright, was the founder and original director of what came to be known as The Soul & Latin Theater.

Maryat scripted our improvised scenes and produced a repertoire of plays focused on three themes: an episode in an inner city classroom, an adolescent homosexual coming out to his parents, and a young addict's unsuccessful attempt at recovery.

As time went on, our plays were in such high demand that we took them from the conventional indoor theater at local schools to the people in the streets. We traveled throughout the city, performing our plays on a custom-built mobile stage complete with sound, lighting, and props.

Not only did we become seasoned actors, but we also became quite skillful at incorporating unforeseen disruptions in our live performances, like water balloons, hecklers, stray dogs, and drunks coming onstage. We went on to perform in upstate New York, New Jersey, and Connecticut and received rave reviews from the *New York Times* and the *Village Voice*.

While Maryat dedicated herself to coordinating the project and writing plays, the task of directing went to Victor Bumbalo and later Clay Stevenson. Victor was a tiny young guy with a gargantuan spirit and avidity for the dramatic arts. A no-nonsense coach with high expectations, he made us work hard towards them.

Clay was a chain-smoking Black actor, director, and dancer who had received training in Europe and ran his own acting studio in the East Village. I had tremendous respect for Clay, a man who had been through the school of hard knocks and who passed on his unbridled passion for perfection and love for the dramatic arts to us.

He was instrumental in acquiring a collection of Miguel Piñero's revolutionary poetry and brilliantly trained us to act them out as a group and in solo performances. We had the privilege once of performing Piñero's poetry at Sing Sing prison while he was still incarcerated there, to the delight of Mr. Piñero and a thunderous ovation from the inmates.

Our experiences were as colorful and diverse as were the members of the troupe. For the first time, I was confronted with the issue of homosexuality and gained the beginnings of understanding and acceptance, albeit on a very basic, unsophisticated level. The only gay I was familiar with was a flamboyant, skinny-as-a-beanpole, middle-aged, excruciatingly ugly wannabe singer named Le Frisón, who often appeared on Mirta Silva's Show.

I realized that Tess, one of the actors, was gay because she was in a relationship with Gerri, a thin, quiet girl who dressed like a boy.

Gerri accompanied Tess to a weekend of performances in an upscale town in New Jersey. We stayed overnight as guests of a local prominent theater buff at his palatial rustic home in the country. Our fine host had invited several of his affluent friends to meet us, and the lot of us had a great time rubbing elbows with the rich folks while partaking of their expensive wine and tasty canapés, though the difference between them and us was clear to see.

Most of us had never been to anything fancier than McDonald's. Louie was in a corner chatting with a lady with his mouth full of hors d'oeuvres. Shorty was in the middle of the room dancing a sexy mambo with a tipsy female. Lefty had spilled some wine on the plush rug and was trying to mop it up with a fancy linen serviette.

What got me snickering was when a gentleman approached Gerri for some light conversation.

"So what's your name, young man?" he asked.

"Gerri," she answered, almost in a whisper.

"My, aren't you shy!" said the gentleman, still with foot in mouth.

"Yes, he is," answered Tess, as she whisked Gerri away before truth be known.

Late that night, as the party guests drank themselves into a stupor, I retired to the loft, ready for bed. I noticed someone had built a makeshift tent with sheets hanging from a ceiling raft, and there was movement inside. As I got closer, a small lamp on the floor inside the tent highlighted against the sheet the silhouette of two people clinging to each other.

Curious to see who was getting frisky in there, I quietly lay on the floor and shoved my head under the hanging sheet. There was Tess in her undies and Gerri in her men's tank undershirt in a lip lock, too engrossed to notice the bodiless head on the floor, peering under the sheet. I just thought, *Oops*, and went about my business without giving it another thought.

Tony joined our troupe soon after we got our very own place in a storefront on 104th Street in El Barrio. He was a nineteen-year-old kid from the neighborhood, skinny as a rail but powerfully strong and solid from years of karate training, which had earned him a black belt in martial arts.

Despite his oppressive upbringing in the rough streets of El Barrio, Tony was gentle and caring and giving. He was a throwaway, deprived and misguided, yet it was these very elements that unleashed the raw emotions and power which lent realism to the characters he portrayed.

Tony brilliantly choreographed a touching dramatic piece set to Isaac Hayes' haunting rendition of "Walk On By." It was magical watching him glide gracefully across the stage with the agile movements of a seasoned dancer.

But his greatest role was that of Louie, the tormented young drug addict in *Dope!* In the play, after seeing his sister fall prey to a ruthless dope peddler, Louie tries to free himself of his addiction for his sister's sake, only to find himself in a deadly confrontation with his pusher. In the end, Louie loses his battle and dies at the hands of a vindictive drug dealer.

I could easily see why Wanda would fall madly in love with Tony. He was a good friend, sweet and kindhearted and mature beyond his years. I never saw Wanda as happy as when she was with Tony.

In an enigmatic twist of fate, and unbeknown to many of us, Tony was, in fact, a heroin addict. When we learned of his addiction, I found it difficult to fathom how he managed to act normally, as my perception of a junkie came from seeing disheveled people on street corners leaning against thin air or semi-stooped with eyes closed and mouths open. I never saw Tony in that position.

Being somewhat naïve about these things, it didn't faze my sister, and she continued to have a relationship with him. But our savvier members and directors became very concerned, as we all cared deeply for Tony and thought he had a very promising future.

Maryat Lee, John our stage manager, and I sat with Tony one day and told him that if he wanted to stay with the group, he needed to get clean.

"We'll help you in any way we can," Maryat said, "but I'm afraid we can't allow this situation to continue. John has found a wonderful rehab for you and our promise to you is that we will allow you to return when you have finished the program."

Without hesitation, Tony replied, "I'll do it. The troupe means everything to me."

We continued to perform with a stand-in playing the part of Louie while Tony went through a rigorous recovery program. Not only that, but we were ecstatic to learn that he had signed up to take exams for acceptance into a GED program.

We welcomed Tony back with open arms, but always unobtrusively vigilant to any signs of relapse. The spirited streets of El Barrio could be very deceiving, with demonic pushers waiting like vultures to pounce on the vulnerable, but especially on the weakness of those who dared to break free of the chains of addiction.

It was Saturday morning, time for house cleaning and our biweekly shopping excursion to La Marqueta with Grandma. Mother had just given me a good sounding after finding an open pack of Marlboros in my schoolbag. I cleverly blamed it on Louie Cheese, a fellow actor, for having left it there.

The phone rang just in time to stop Mother's barrage of annoying questions, and I quickly picked it up. It was John, our manager.

"Hey John, what's up? Someone rip off our speakers again?" I was a bit annoyed that he was calling as we had just had a falling out the day before.

"No, no it's not that," he said solemnly. "I have something to tell you."

"Oh, boy. Okay, let me have it." There was a long pause on the other end. "John?"

"Tony's dead."

"What did you just say?" I asked, the words coming out in slow motion.

"Tony's dead. His friend Ronnie found him last night and…."

This can't be real, I thought. This is not happening. I remember feeling the numbness, like protective armor, begin to shut down my brain, my spirit of any emotion, except for one thought…Wanda.

"Hello…Isabel…are you still there?"

I don't know how long he was talking, but I asked him to tell me again what had happened to Tony.

"Ronnie went to see Tony at the apartment last night. He said the door was open. He walked right in and found Tony on his bed, unconscious. By the time the ambulance got there, Tony was gone. I don't know if he did it on purpose or if it was an accident, but apparently he OD'd on heroin."

A sharp pain hit me in my midsection as his cutting words pierced the veneer that shielded my grief, and out flowed the pain in silent tears. I didn't want my sister to see me crying.

"Thanks, John. We'll talk again later, okay?" I barely got the words out.

"Sure thing. I'm sorry, Isabel. Tell your sister I'm really sorry about what's happened."

Tell Wanda. How do I tell Wanda?

I took a few moments to compose myself and then went in search of my sister. She was sitting on the fire escape, looking straight ahead with a blank stare. As I quietly climbed out the window and sat next to her, I knew in an instant that she knew. She must have overheard all or part of my conversation with John.

No words were spoken. I put my arm around her shoulders, but she didn't respond. She just sat there, staring straight ahead.

Tony's service was held two days later at Ortiz's Funeral Home on 103rd Street. His story was reported in the *New York Time, El Diario-La Prensa,* and in the nightly TV news. "Actor, 19, Who Plays Addict, Dies of Narcotic Overdose" read the headlines.

On the day of his burial, actress Estelle Parsons read a beautiful poem written by Maryat Lee honoring Tony's life. It wasn't until we said our final good-byes that I saw my sister finally cave in to her grief.

We all rode together in Maryat's van to St. Raymond's Cemetery, and all through the ride there and back, Miss Parsons held my sister in her arms as she forlornly gazed out the window at the streets where Tony had once lived and danced and loved.

Ironically, it was while I was a member of the theater troupe that I found my voice. Inspired by very assertive group members who had no qualms about speaking their minds, and encouraged by my newfound ability to perform in public, I became passionately outspoken about some of the social issues that confronted us during this impactful period of social unrest. I no longer sat on the sidelines and watched the parade go by but took an active interest in the problems that affected my community and my people, and I joined the procession.

The years 1967 through 1970 marked an unparalleled era of social and political activism spurred on by anger, frustration, and a deep sense of injustice against the political machinery, prompting people to take to the streets and let their voices be heard. I rallied against the war in Vietnam, not to spew hatred against the men and women who served there, but to urge politicians to stop the insanity and bring our soldiers home. I spoke up for political prisoners and joined the war against poverty. When the Young Lords held a rally or a protest march, I was there.

Of course, Mother was never informed of where I was going, for as much as I wanted to make grown-up choices, I was still a woman-child under her thumb.

In the late sixties, we moved yet again, this time to a swarming tenement on East 153rd Street in the South Bronx. Another two-bedroom railroad flat, this one was on the third floor and faced the front of the building. A bedroom faced the street, and at night, we would lean on a pillow on the windowsill and take in all that was going on below.

The narrow, cobbled street was a small community onto itself with people hanging off fire escapes and spilling out onto the stoops in the summer. Honking cars and ambulances with blaring sirens raced by. Mr. Softee's ice cream truck announced its arrival with its familiar chiming jingle.

Fire hydrants were opened, and its whooshing sound was met by children's joyful squeals as they played and cooled themselves off in the rushing water. One rascal would inevitably take a hollow tin can, place it near the mouth of the hydrant, make the water rise higher, and give out free car washes, whether the driver wanted one or not.

When it was really hot outside, some people found refuge up on the roof, where they could feel the warm summer breeze and watch the stars come out at night.

In the winter, the street was as desolate and quiet as an arctic tundra. Inside, my mother would bang on the radiators and pipes for some heat and hot water. Some practices never changed.

Cousin Louie and his parents moved directly across the street, and even though he lived up on the sixth floor, we could still yell out the window at each other, which is what everyone else seemed to do.

The bad part was that Uncle Anibal's weekend binges continued, and so did his manic contempt for Mother. Sometimes his wife became the target of his drunken aggression. "Josefinaaaaaaa, open the door, you dirty whore!"

The other ugly part was that the dreaded wicked witches, Conchita and Gina, also lived across the street and were, in fact, responsible for enticing Mother to move to the same block. Now the gossip flew back and forth like shuttlecocks across a badminton court.

That's where I met Millie, a cute munchkin with a gap between her teeth, who lived across the hall from us. At seventeen, Millie was only a year older than me, but her parents let her go to dances and parties, a privilege I very much envied. She had a passion for Latin music, and I owe her honors for having patiently and expertly taught me how to dance salsa.

Once I learned the moves that went with the rhythms of the congas and timbales, I was hooked. Although I continued to listen to American pop music, it was the sublime pulsation of the Latin beat that triggered an almost unconscious compelling need to move to the music with total abandon.

There isn't a dance that can compare to the gaiety, the timing and cohesiveness of hand maneuvers, the provocative movements in unison of an upbeat salsa dance. The sweating, the writhing bodies, the facial expressions; the start of a moderate sensual beat, climaxing in the middle to a crescendo and ending with a slower consummation is like making love in its most exquisite form. Of course, at sixteen I didn't know what making love was, but time and experience would prove it to be so.

Wanda and I continued to perform with the theater troupe, but this time, I was paid a small wage for doing secretarial work in our new storefront on 104th Street. Still, the money was not enough to buy the things I needed for school, and Mother's public assistance check was barely enough to cover the rent and utilities and food to feed us all.

Although Grandma was ingenious at making a dollar go a long way on our biweekly shopping excursions to La Marqueta, there were days when all we had was a fried egg over white rice or a bowl of cornmeal for supper.

Our clothes were still handmade on Grandma's antique sewing machine from whatever fabrics were on sale, and most of little Bernie's clothes were hand-me-downs from other families.

It didn't take much to convince my sister that we should go on a buying spree with no money.

Wanda and I boarded a subway headed downtown to Gimbel's on 86th Street, then one of New York's elegant department stores. We were a far cry from the impoverished masses rummaging through cheesy budget clothing that hung from awnings or were displayed in cardboard boxes. Here, the aroma of fresh pretzels mingled with the scent of L'Air du Temps as crowds of sophisticated New Yorkers made their way through the revolving doors of this infamous shopper's mecca.

We had never been inside Gimbel's though we knew of it. It seemed naively rational that if we were to take anything from anyone, it should be from people who had so much that they wouldn't miss it.

My sister and I spent hours wandering awe-struck through aisle upon aisle of the most exquisite apparel and accessories we had ever seen. Every now and then, our eyes would catch a fine pair of pants or a nice blouse, and into the goody bag it went. We thought of practical things we needed, like underwear and even clothes for our brothers and baby sister, and into the bag they too went.

Unenlightened to the rules of efficient pilfering, of knowing when to stop, and oblivious to the cameras and security personnel around us, we stuffed four bags full of merchandise and cheerfully sauntered through the revolving glass doors.

No sooner had we gotten outside, two burly men in street clothes grabbed our bags and our arms. The sudden maneuver was startling.

"What are you doing? What is this?" I yelled at the bulldog with the pincer grip on my arm.

"What the hell do you think this is, you stupid spic?" he yelled back. The use of that dehumanizing word was even more shocking to me than the realization that we had gotten caught.

They bulldozed us into a busy back room and made us sit on a bench while they took inventory of the items we had taken. Not knowing what fate awaited us, Wanda and I started to cry. Would we be arrested and sent to jail? Even worse, were they going to tell Mother? I would rather they send us away on a life sentence to Alcatraz than face Mother's wrath. Wanda and I started to cry even harder.

A short while later, we were ushered into a back office to face an official seated behind a huge desk. In front of him was the pile of clothes we had taken: the beautiful blouses, the nice shoes, the pant and shirt sets for our brothers, the toddler clothes for little Bernadette and, most embarrassing, the teen bras and underwear we had chosen for ourselves. Oddly enough, the gentleman addressed us in a soft, kind voice.

"Who were these things for?" he asked.

"Well...some of it for us, some for our brothers and sister," I answered as I wiped away a tear. I cried, not because I was frightened, but because I was disappointed that we wouldn't be able to surprise our siblings with the "gifts" we had gotten.

He paused for a minute. "You two look like nice girls. Have you ever done this before?"

"No, sir," I whimpered.

"Well, I tell you what. I'll speak to the store manager about not filing charges, but you must promise me that you will never, ever do this again."

"Yes, sir. We promise," Wanda and I stammered in unison.

It was a valuable lesson learned. If ever we wanted or needed anything, we would have to work for it. No matter how noble or unselfish our wants or needs were, we could never rely on shortcuts unless we were prepared to deal with repercussions and to take responsibility for our actions. We never lost sight of that lesson.

9

Taking Chances

I entered my senior year of high school in the fall of 1969. I was in a college-bound program where kids with decent grades were groomed with college-level courses and received guidance in choosing and applying to various colleges. I tried to do my best academically, not just because I wanted to eventually go on to medical school and make Grandma proud, but because it was the door to a world beyond the suffocating boundaries of my stale life.

There wasn't a conscious effort to intellectualize or rationalize why I wanted to move away but a gut feeling, a burning desire to seek out something better, to see what lay beyond the confines of my barrio. I wanted my own space, my own things; to think on my own and make my own decisions; to fall in love, have friends, and experience life without unreasonable rules and unrealistic time constraints. I wanted to be free.

I was sick and tired of looking out the window and seeing the time-worn emaciated ruins that reeked of hunger and despair; sick of roaches and mice and other assorted vermin sharing our living space; of cracked, litter-strewn sidewalks lined with dope peddlers and lecherous men calling out lascivious remarks to young girls; of the suffocating masses living atop one another amidst the maddening clamor of an insomnious city.

Through reading, I had become aware of an unexplored world beyond the box, one that beckoned with new adventures, different perspectives, and choices for a better life that were mine for the taking if I stayed focused and driven.

I began to research different schools, concentrating on those that were far enough from the city where I couldn't commute every day but near enough so that I could visit without having to pay a fortune for travel. A few of the smarter kids were applying to Ivy League schools, and the rest were handed city college applications, as if they didn't have a choice.

I settled on the University of Connecticut for its fine academics and beautiful campus. It was also conveniently distant from the South Bronx and Mother's watchful eye. I made an appointment to see my guidance counselor, Mr. Schlanger, to tell him about my choice.

"You'll never get into that school. Your grades aren't good enough," he said.

"I'm going to apply anyway," I said.

"Well, just in case, here's a city college application."

I took the application home and never looked at it. Instead, I headed straight for the library, did some more research on the university, and found the names of two advisors who dealt specifically with the recruitment of minority students.

Although equal opportunity and affirmative action laws had been passed years earlier, the early seventies saw a quasi-moral commitment to implementing these laws, particularly in education. Whether it was due to lawmakers finally gaining a conscience or the pervasive threat of frustrated and angry Latinos and Blacks threatening the infrastructure with rallies, riots and takeovers, I couldn't say. I seized the opportunity and immediately wrote to the school's recruiters, telling them about my circumstances, my goals and dreams.

I told Mother and Grandma about my plans to go away to college, and they took it quite well. For them, it was not about my accomplishments being rewarded or being the first in the family to go to college. Neither Mother nor Grandma had gone past elementary school education, and the concept of such an achievement and the commitment and work that would follow was neither measurable nor fathomable to them. They just knew that I was going away to be a doctor, and that's what Mother told all her friends and relatives.

"So what kind of doctor are you going to be?" hissed Gina, the green-eyed viper.

"Oh, I don't know—a brain surgeon?" I retorted.

"What does a brain surgeon do? Look at brains and cut out the crazy parts?" she asked.

"Yes, and you'll be my first patient," I retaliated. I looked at Mother, and she gave me the cold dagger glare.

On a beautiful sunny weekend in May, two of my high school buddies and I boarded a Greyhound bus to Storrs for an open house event. I was ecstatic about going to see what could possibly be my new home for the next four years.

Steel and concrete slowly metamorphosed into open highways and finally into a lush country road with lavish corpulent trees, their overhanging branches forming awnings over the winding roads as we approached the university grounds.

The bus stopped in front of the campus' row of rustic shops, which included a pharmacy, a bookstore, a quaint clothing shop for girls, and a large café. Across the enface two-lane road was a large duck pond surrounded by blooming trees and skirted by several two-story modern buildings which housed some of the classrooms. English ivy crawled up the façade of some of the older buildings, giving them the distinguished look of old academia. I had reached my Walden Pond.

We met with the recruiters I had contacted, who graciously gave us a tour of the grounds and spent time talking to us about the school and its academic offerings. I needed no convincing, and I'm sure that my enthusiasm was quite evident.

We also met two of the four Hispanic students enrolled out of a total student population of 30,000. Although the number of Latinos there was disheartening, to say the least, it did not dissuade me from applying.

I learned from the recruiters that they had a decent number of Black students, most of whom lived in a quad of dorms nicknamed "the jungle." Whereas many of my class-mates chose to remain within the comfort zone of their neighborhoods, I was not intimidated by the challenge of being a true minority in a class of people about whom I knew very little. The fact that there were other minority students there, albeit a small number, was good enough for me.

I went back home, carefully filled out my application, and mailed it. I kept in touch with the two Hispanic students I had met, Carmen and Ino, and made plans to room with Carmen should I get accepted. I also stayed in touch with the two advisors, asking questions and showing interest while unobtrusively making sure that they didn't forget me.

The letter came a few weeks later. I was accepted, and so were my buddies, Brunie and Norma.

I took that acceptance letter and, smiling from ear to ear, showed it to Mr. Schlanger the next morning. He was in ut-ter disbelief and sheepishly congratulated me. On my 1970 yearbook, he wrote, "Dear Isabel, I wish you all the best in your future, which I am sure will be most interesting." Those words would prove to be an understatement.

The day finally arrived when I would leave home and embark on an exciting new adventure full of promise. Most importantly, I was going to be free—free to explore, to be myself, to grow without encumbrances or limitations.

I cheerfully packed my worldly possessions into card-board boxes, including my trusty Japanese camera. Grandma carefully filled a box with some of my favorite food items: boxes of cornmeal and cereal, bags of rice and coffee, cans of beans and soup, six-packs of malta beverages, and bunches of green plantains and bananas.

As Uncle Carlos stuffed my belongings into his old station wagon, it suddenly dawned on me that while I was preparing to move on with my life, I was leaving behind my Grandma and brothers and sisters. I tearfully hugged each one and promised that I would visit as often as I could.

Mother accompanied me and Uncle Carlos on the 3 ½ hour journey to Storrs, and once there, I could tell that she was impressed with the beauty and serenity of the university grounds. Carmen, my new roommate, and Ino were waiting for me in the dorm, a three-story building with pristine hallways, modern amenities, and small but adequate rooms.

I was mesmerized—no peeling paint, no litter, no roaches sharing the food. There was a small kitchenette where I could prepare my rice and beans on a stove that didn't need matches to light the burners. There were no bathtubs but spotlessly clean showers, and the toilets had a handle to flush rather than a string hanging from a box above the seat.

A beautifully decorated, carpeted lounge was on the second floor where I could quietly study, with floor to ceiling windows overlooking the grassy knolls and verdant landscape. No sounds of police sirens or people yelling could be heard, only the pleasing melodious chirping of song sparrows. The first few nights there were so quiet, I thought I was going deaf.

I quickly said my good-byes to Mother and Uncle Carlos, then wasted no time in unpacking and taking a stroll through the campus with Carmen and Ino. I had them show me first and foremost the library and made a mental map of its location. We went in search of my friends, Norma and Brunie, who had been assigned rooms in "the jungle" dorms on the opposite end of the campus, much to their delight.

It was 1970, a year that marked the height of student protests on campuses across the nation. Educational activism by minority students sought to address historical inequities in access to higher education and relevant curriculums specific to the Black and Hispanic experience.

I became aware that stringent admissions policies did not take into consideration the substandard education and preparation that many inner city students received and that, once accepted, there were no transitional programs to help us catch up with the general student population.

Thus, many minority students were prone to drop out, adding to a sense of failure. It was up to those of us with a foot in academia's door to help other disadvantaged students by raising our voices and, in turn, stirring the collective consciousness of the policymakers in higher education.

It was, indeed, a noble cause, and one that I embraced passionately and unswervingly. Much later, I would learn that it was a two-way street, and that one can lead the proverbial horse to water but cannot make it drink.

My first year at the university was a whirlwind hodge-podge of classes, sociopolitical activities, and the fading echoes of lost musical icons. In the first month of my fresh-man year, I learned via a radio broadcast that my favorite rock guitarist, Jimi Hendrix, had died, and a month later, my idol, Janis Joplin, had also succumbed to drugs. It symboli-cally marked a transition for me from peaceful, bead-wear-ing hippie to outspoken radical.

Sometime in the spring of the following year, I came across an interesting announcement in a local New York City newspaper. Applications were being sought from mi-nority undergraduates to attend a special program at Har-vard University for pre-med students.

It was a chance of a lifetime, but would I qualify? Was I good enough, and did I have what it took to compete with Harvard's highbrow prodigies? Would I be able to handle the disappointment if I didn't get accepted?

I vacillated for a few days until I realized that I was being unfair in denying myself a fighting chance for this golden opportunity. Why not me? What would be the worst that could happen?

Once again, I took a chance and filled out an application, wrote the required essay, and sent the package, complete with sweaty fingerprints.

Two months later, I received their reply. I was in.

10

Harvard with a Dash of Sofrito

Mother had received a notice that the building we lived in was being demolished to build a high-rise project in its place. She finally got her wish to live in a city housing project, and we were temporarily relocated to a rundown building on 143rd Street in the South Bronx.

I had no sooner gotten home for summer break before I packed again and made my way to Harvard. Dorothy had reached the Land of Oz. I was too excited and awestruck to feel any fear.

My dorm room was in Weld Hall, an archaic brick structure built in 1870, facing what is now referred to as the old Harvard Yard. I carried my worn suitcase and paper shopping bag brimming with the goodies Grandma had packed, up the front steps, past the double archways, and up the wide staircase to my room on the fourth floor.

I stopped for a few minutes to catch my breath, and in that moment, I reverted to my old habit of time traveling through the richly descriptive scenes of a classic historic novel. I pictured the Harvard of *The Late George Apley*, where young aristocrats in Prince Albert coats and striped cravats chased giggling girls in crinolines down these stairs, past gilded portraits of somber founding fathers. The sounds of real laughter broke my reverie. I continued to hike up one more flight of stairs to my assigned quarters.

Beyond the suite's front door was an entry foyer with three separate bedrooms. My room was small and sparse with a twin bed against the right wall, an old desk and chair, and a tall window directly opposite the entry doorway.

My own room. This will do very nicely.

I decided to freshen up before attending the orientation meeting and found that the shared bathroom was on the third floor. Although the toilets were private stalls, I was dismayed to find that the showers had no doors, and even though it was an all-girls bathroom, I didn't feel very comfortable about someone walking in on me while in the buff scrubbing my privates.

It was a sultry early evening when I sauntered past old ivy-laden brick buildings full of history to our meeting place in Barker Hall. It was there that I learned I was one of fifty students chosen nationwide for this honor, and for the first time in my life, I felt proud and accomplished.

There were students there representing every minority group—Blacks, Hispanics including two Puerto Ricans from the island, Asian-Americans, and one American Indian. I met two of the Latinos from New York, Ladislao and Heriberto, and a very outspoken Latino from Boston named Jaime. We bonded immediately.

After the orientation session, a group of us met in the old Harvard yard, and sitting under the leafy arms of an old elm tree, we talked and shared stories until there was no one left but us. Our laughter echoed against the façades of the surrounding buildings into the late evening hours.

My first class was biology, which was held in an auditorium-like classroom with other Harvard students. Some of the summer program attendees were there, including Ladislao, Heriberto, and Jaime. The professor in that course had the unfortunate practice of giving monotone robotic lectures full of technical details, just perfect for fighting an early morning snooze.

My second class was chemistry with a very nice Black professor who reminded me of Fred Sanford, the father in the TV sitcom, *Sanford and Son*. Only the summer program students participated in this class, which was small and informal and definitely not conducive to an evening siesta.

As time went on and some of us began to engage in nonacademic extracurricular activities. Professor "Sanford," as good-natured as he was, became exasperated with our nonchalance and let us know, in no uncertain terms, that he would not put up with any shenanigans from us. That's when we buckled down and took our studies seriously, for we sensed that he genuinely cared. From that day on, we made a concerted effort not to disappoint him.

Early on, I learned with great interest that Jaime was a community activist in the Boston area who had ties to the Young Lords Party in New York. He actually lived part-time in a commune-like residence with his wife and three other radicals. A few of us joined him in his efforts and began to conduct door-to-door TB testing on Saturdays and sold the Young Lords' *P'alante* newspapers in the highly populated community of Roxbury.

It was a wonderful hectic summer full of learning, political activism, socializing, and cementing new friendships. It was also the summer I lost my virginity.

I'm embarrassed to say that I don't remember his name, and that's a befitting remark considering that the whole affair was just as forgettable. Truth be told, I had my eye on Ernie, a gorgeous, tall and slender caramel stud muffin with whom I had the pleasure of locking lips while lying on the grass under a star-filled blanket one balmy night. For whatever reason, Ernie resisted my feminine allure, and we remained purely friends after that.

Dejected as I felt, I managed to gently pick up and shield my wounded dignity as I had been down this road before and was not about to dwell on what could have been.

I had received correspondence from my good friends, Norma and Brunie, both of whom had no qualms about openly sharing their experiences with me. Thanks to them, I had already moved beyond my childhood friend Maria's warnings about kissing while having my monthly "friend." According to Maria, babies were just something that magically appeared when you kissed a boy you loved, which is how I imagined my mother had conceived my brothers.

Back in those days, while playing with my sister Wanda and cousin Louie in his apartment, he brought out a deck of cards with shocking pictures of men and women doing odd things with each other's bodies. It was then that I realized sex was a little more than just kissing. This gave me a crude idea of what sex entailed, and without making the connection between romantic feelings, wanton desire for someone, or the electrifying sensations of the act itself, it was not something I eagerly anticipated.

But Norma and Brunie had painted such a stimulating picture of their romantic encounters, I began to wonder what this was all about but in a detached, intellectual way, as if it was something that needed to be dissected and researched to ascertain if there was any truth to their animated stories.

I met him while sitting with friends in the open back of a truck on our way to Jaime's commune in Brookline for drinks and conversation. His quiet, shy disposition was what initially attracted me, though I later found out that he had just arrived from Puerto Rico and knew very little English.

Rico, as I will call him for lack of memory, was not physically striking but was remarkably intelligent when it came to discussing Puerto Rico's history or the political ramifications of statehood versus independence. He held me captive with his knowledge of the imperialist agenda and his involvement in radical groups on the island. With hindsight,

I can see where he used his political expertise to charm my socks off, for had I relied on looks alone, we would have never connected.

The second time we met was under the old elm tree in Harvard Yard where a group of us was shooting the breeze, drinking wine, and having a good laugh. We talked until there was no one left but the two of us, and conveniently not having a ride back to his cousin's apartment, I invited him to stay with me. I honestly thought he would be a gentleman and not try anything but, of course, he did.

I let him have his way out of sheer curiosity—I was finally going to find out what all the hoopla was about.

The minute the lights went out, he jumped on me like a dog in heat. I stopped him for a second to let him know that I was still a virgin, which should have clued him in to be more civilized, but instead, it made the uncultivated beast even more ferocious, as if the prized fruit would fall off if he didn't hurry.

I would love to enthrall you with titillating details of what followed, but there aren't any. It was straightforward, on and off, without passion or emotion, no creative poses or whispered sweet nothings. It was the most awkward, primitive experience I'd ever had since my first kiss, and it left me thinking that this sex thing was way overrated.

He kept clinging to me like a baby baboon clings to its mother's back, always touching and wanting to kiss whenever and wherever the urge hit him, which was oftentimes embarrassing.

I began to develop animosity towards him verging on contempt, for I realized that he had manipulated me, and I had foolishly made a very poor choice. The more I pushed him away, the more he insisted on being with me. I finally had enough of him, and in one defining moment, I let him know, in no uncertain terms, that he needed to move on and, reluctantly, he did.

As the summer drew to its end and the students began to return home, Ladislao and I decided to continue our work in the community. We moved into Jaime's commune until it was time to return to our respective colleges in the fall.

While there, we met with a Young Lords Party member, who conducted informal lectures on socialist reform and discussed pertinent quotations from Mao Tse-Tung's, *The Little Red Book*. It was then that I discovered the socially relevant satirical poetry of Pedro Pietri and learned the difference between the bourgeoisie and the lumpen proletariat according to Marxist ideology.

In my idealistic mind, I became immersed in their rhetoric because I believed that this was a viable solution to our community's problems. It wasn't until a Young Lords minister told me that I could better serve my people by leaving school for now and committing myself totally to the cause, that I decided remaining with the Party was not in my best interest.

I returned to UConn in the fall and completely immersed myself in furthering the cause of Latino students' rights. Carmen, Ino, Brunie, Norma, and I rounded up most of the new students and went to great lengths to encourage them to join our cause. Unfortunately, as time went on, we realized that many were more interested in partying and hooking up in their free time than becoming involved in our laborious progressive agenda.

It was amazing how much our small group managed to accomplish in a short period of time. We took over a small warehouse used to store the theater department's props and costumes and turned it into our cultural center, La Casa Borinqueña.

At one point, we politely set up a meeting with the university's provost, then took over his office and demanded funds for our projects. The provost wasn't impressed with our approach but coolly agreed to our requests.

With a grant from the university in hand, I traveled to New York and bought dozens of wonderful books on Puerto Rican history, culture, and literature to stock our new library.

I gave seminars around campus on the Puerto Ricans' political and economic crises on the island and in the states and on the role of Puerto Rican women in society.

We organized Puerto Rican History Week and invited Hispanic scholars and writers to give informal talks and lectures. I was very pleased to see that these informative sessions were well attended and that a large portion of the attendees were our own professors and other non-Hispanic students. It was encouraging to see others take an interest in our culture and want to learn more about us for that was one of our aims.

One day was set aside to honor our parents with a tour of the university, followed by dinner and a comedy show mimicking our parents' mannerisms. It was worth every ounce of sweat to hear my mother's laughter in the audience.

I was proud of our accomplishments, but my tireless work took a detrimental toll on my studies. I finished the fall semester with disastrous grades.

I returned home for winter recess, looking forward to some much needed rest and a chance to spend quality time with my family during my favorite time of the year. No matter where I went, it could never compare to the gaiety in my family's home.

Mother's apartment was brimming with holiday decorations. There in the corner of the living room was the old artificial tree laden with bangles and baubles and tinsel weighing down its emaciated branches. Greeting cards hung from strings across a wall, and Christmas lights flickered on and off on the frosted windows behind Grandma's forest of overgrown house plants.

It was loud and noisy with the radio blasting Spanish music and my little brothers and sister running amok amidst the tightly packed furniture, but it was also cozy and familiar.

A large pot simmered noisily on the old stove while Grandma prepared a heavenly brew of Bustelo because she knew how much I loved her coffee. I sat at the kitchen table, covered with a plastic holiday tablecloth, and reached for a slice of buttered bread.

"Hey, Isabel, I've got something to tell you," said Wanda with a radiant smile on her face. This better be good, I thought. The last time she said that, I got a baby sister. I swallowed the tasty morsel, licked my fingers, and gave her my full attention.

"I'm getting married," she said.

"What? When did this happen?" I asked dumbfounded, like it was a done deal. She was only eighteen years old, for crissakes! And where was Mother when all this happened? She allowed her to date this guy? How did I miss all of this?

"Well, his name is Sammy, and he's a really nice guy, Sis. He has his own place and has a good job and no bad habits, and he's very good to me. I can't wait for you to meet him. I know you're gonna like him."

Her eyes sparkled as she spoke of him and my heart melted for her. There was no way I was going to dampen her spirits with my cynical inquiries. I just hoped that she wasn't impulsively taking this big step just to get out of the house.

I asked Mother privately how this all came about, and she sighed and replied with resignation, "I'd rather she get married than run around behind my back making babies."

Wanda had mentioned that his nickname was Tirito, Spanish for "little bullet," and one look at him later that afternoon, and I could see why. He was a tiny gnome, an inch shorter than my sister, with a Chia pet curly 'fro, a wide smile, and a deep dimple in his chin.

In Spanish we have a saying: "Para los gustos hicieron los colores," meaning loosely "to each his own." I decided to go beyond the looks and get to know him a little.

Apparently he had come to the mainland from Puerto Rico not long before he met my sister and spoke just enough English to get by. He was shy and charming. With a soft voice, he told me about his background, his parents back home, and his plans for the future.

Later in the evening, he took me into a bedroom with my sister, where he nervously professed his love for her and told me he wanted to marry her.

He was a winner! I zealously hugged them and welcomed him to the family.

It was Christmas Eve and the tiny apartment quickly filled with family and friends. Cousin Louie came from across the street with Uncle Anibal and his wife, Josefina; cousins Edwin and Carlos came with Uncle Carlos and wife Migue; my childhood friend, Chachi, was there with her brothers and her mother, Margot; and of course, the heathens Gina and Conchita came to appraise the food and gather newsworthy gossip.

Friends we hadn't seen in years showed up, a custom that took place every year to our great delight. The mirth was deafening, the savory food plentiful, the music upbeat and loud. This year we celebrated with even more gusto as we announced my sister's engagement to Sammy.

After one glass of rum-spiked coquito secretly slurped in the back bedroom, I became lightheaded and loose-tongued. By now, Uncle Anibal had had a few beers, drunken meter fast approaching danger zone. Suddenly, my brother Edwin darted across the living room chasing after little Bernadette.

"Mani, hey Mani, come here," he called out to my brother.

"Why are you calling him Mani?" I asked him.

"Mani, you know, manicomio," he taunted, and everyone started to laugh. Manicomio is Spanish for insane asylum. I was livid!

"Don't you dare ever call him that again!" I shouted at him. "You keep doing that, and you'll be responsible for my brother growing up thinking that he's crazy. What's your excuse for being a drunk?"

With that, Mother grabbed me by my arm, dragged me to the bedroom, and gave me a good sounding for being disrespectful to Uncle Anibal.

Late that night, after everyone had gone home and we were all tucked in and sleeping, I was awakened by a very familiar voice crying from the street below. "Josefinaaaaa, open the door goddammit. I'm freezing!"

Oh Lord, she locked him out again.

My sister and Sammy were married in the spring of 1972 in a very simple ceremony held at the same church where we had done our first communion. Sammy got homesick and decided to take his new bride back home to Naranjito, a tiny town in Puerto Rico hidden high up in the mountains. I cried my eyes out for days after they left.

I returned to the university and continued to work tirelessly with my fellow activists to keep the center running while making an earnest effort to maintain good grades. One course in particular proved to be my undoing and challenged my ultimate goal and my sanity.

Comparative Vertebrae Anatomy was a prerequisite in the pre-med course of study. In that class, I was able to dissect the little frog and prick its nerve to watch its little leg jump. I managed to slice up the big fish and describe its innards in detail. But I had a serious problem when the professor presented a dead cat to each of us as our next project. It was revolting, but I forged ahead with one eye closed.

I painstakingly began to skin the unfortunate puss and was still removing the skin when others were already identifying the muscles. Evidently, I was progressing too slowly for the professor, who came to my table, and in one fell swoop, skinned the poor thing as I cringed in disgust.

I glanced at the stiff animal out of the corner of my eye and knew I could not carry out the rest of my assignment. There was no way I could continue to cut up that unlucky dear, even if he was dead as a doornail.

I scrubbed the stench of formaldehyde off my hands and returned to my dorm, resigned to accept a failing grade. It was now clear that I needed to re-evaluate my waning commitment to become a doctor in view of this recent failure and my growing interest in sociopolitical activism.

Things happen for a reason, an overused cliché but one saturated with truth. My life was to be shaped by ironies and coincidences, both good and bad, which defied explanation but would eventually reveal their definitive purpose.

For me, it was all about taking chances when unforeseen situations presented themselves that had the potential of leading me to something bigger and better. Whether or not I had the right background, the right credentials, the right attitude were all moot points. I could accept a rejection, but I could never accept the regret of not having tried.

One day while eyeing the bulletin board in the cafeteria, I came across an announcement for applications to the Junior Year Abroad in France Program.

Imagine the possibilities! A poor girl from the tenements of El Barrio and the South Bronx studying in Paris. The thought made my toes curl.

Wondering if my years of junior and senior high school French would qualify me, I quickly scanned the fine print for requirements. Not having found any that would exclude me for consideration, I made a beeline for the French Department and picked up an application with fantasies of strolling through Simone de Beauvoir's Parisian streets swirling in my head.

I filled it out and wrote a heartfelt essay while preparing myself for a rejection. The program was probably intended for French majors, but I just had to give it a shot.

Meanwhile, I continued to study hard and work even harder at the Puerto Rican Center. We managed to motivate a core group of Latino students to form an association that would continue the work that we had started. However, much to our frustration, there were others we could not reach. Unable to juggle social and academic activities, many started dropping out of the university like flies.

A month later, I opened my mailbox—and there it was. A letter from the French Department. I took the envelope to the privacy of my dorm room in case I needed to cry. Very carefully and with hands shaking, I tore it open and unfolded the letter.

Dear Miss Lopez:

Congratulations! You have passed our initial review of your application and we would like to schedule you for the interview portion on...

Oh, I couldn't believe it! Paris, the beautiful city I had envisioned through novels and pictures from travel magazines. The idea that I was being given a chance, that I could possibly be one of the lucky ones, that I could actually see Paris, was mindboggling. What words could I use to make them understand where I came from and why this meant so much to me?

I visualized myself time and again sitting in front of the interviewer and confidently telling him or her about myself and why I wanted to study in Paris without sounding too pathetic.

On the day of the interview, I rummaged through my closet for my most appropriate bohemian attire, and with a smile glued on my face to hide the nervous tic, I made my way to the French Department, pumping myself up all the way there.

I met with Professor Bartow, the program director, who eerily bore a striking resemblance to Abe Lincoln but without the pockmarks. He greeted me with a welcoming smile, a warm handshake, and courteously offered me a seat.

Luckily, I was asked the questions I expected, and as the interview progressed, it became more of a casual conversation than an interview. Maybe he'd noticed the tic.

Professor Bartow went on to inform me that the students would be in Paris for a three week orientation with introductory courses in literature and French conversation. Following that, students would travel to Rouen in Normandy, where they would be placed with families while they attended the university there.

"How would you feel about being placed with an older couple?" he asked. I immediately thought of my beautiful grandmother.

"I'd be delighted. They would probably have wonderful stories to tell about their younger years and have a greater appreciation for the history of their birthplace. I could learn a lot from them," I responded. He smiled. *Good answer.*

Mr. Bartow prepared his next question. "You know, the French people love their food and have certain unusual delicacies that might be offered to you, which you would be expected to try. How would you feel about eating, say, sautéed frog legs or snails or broiled cow tongue?" The look of shock he probably expected never came.

"Well sir, in my culture, we have delicacies too, like morcilla which is intestines stuffed with a mix of spicy rice and dry blood, or toallas, which is the lining of a cow's stomach cooked in a tasty sauce or served in hearty soups. So the frog legs don't sound too bad as long as they're not attached to the frog." He laughed. *Good sign.*

The interview ended on an upbeat note, and I left with a good feeling that soon gave way to nerve-racking uncertainty.

A week later, I received the envelope. The response came much too soon for it to be positive news. I held the envelope in my sweaty hands and mentally prepared myself for the possibility of disappointment. After all, there were many French majors who probably applied and had better qualifications and a greater vested interest than I. Oh, well. I had given it a shot, and maybe someday I could visit on my own.

I carefully opened the envelope and unfolded the letter as I held my breath.

Dear Miss Lopez:

After careful review of your application to the Junior Year Abroad in France Program, Dr. Bartow and the Program Review Panel are pleased to extend our congratulations on your acceptance into the...

I was going to France! I screamed, I cried, I dreamed and planned. I told everyone—friends and family and any stranger who would listen. My spirits were high up in the clouds long before I got on the plane. I was going to France!

For the remainder of that spring semester, I attended an orientation course where I immersed myself in everything French, reading and learning about their history, culture, and language. There, I met the other thirty-nine students that had been chosen. I was the only minority member in the group.

As we were to be paired off, I chose to ask a bubbly, life-size Cabbage Patch clone named Debbie to be my roommate, and she agreed.

I returned home that summer, excited about my upcoming journey and ready to tell my family the news that I had changed my mind about becoming a doctor. I wasn't sure what direction my life would take, but I knew that this incredible opportunity could not be missed.

Mother and Grandma took my decision quite well, softened by the good news and the pitiful guilt-filled sobbing I had mastered through the years to get out of trouble.

11

Friends, Lovers, Creeps, and Other Strangers

I needed to find summer work, and somewhere in the back of my mind, I remembered a Job Corps office back in El Barrio that helped students find temporary employment. It was there, while filling out an application, that I saw him.

Tall, lanky, with an unruly mophead of curly black hair and a cigarette dangling from his lips was the finest looking Latino specimen of manhood that I had seen in a long time. Our eyes met briefly, and he smiled, somehow managing to keep the burning cigarette attached to the side of his mouth. It gave him the sensual allure of a 1940s film noir star.

With heart racing and hand shaking, I finished scribbling my life history on the application and handed it in. Not long afterwards, my name was called, and I was escorted to a back office. There, sitting behind a desk piled with paperwork and an ashtray full of butts, was the Latino Adonis.

"Hi! My name is Frankie, and I'm one of the job counselors here. How are you today?" His smile was electrifying.

"Great, just great," I managed to answer.

He asked me a few questions about my application and what I was looking for. Each of us had a knack for coming up with humorous remarks, and before long, we were having a lively conversation with a few wisecracks thrown in and a lot of laughter. He was not only handsome and intelligent, but funny too.

"Well, Isabel, let me go through our job listings and see if there's anything suitable for you. Let's make an appointment for you to come back on Friday at about 4:00 p.m. I should have some information for you by then." Friday, just two more days.

"Sure, I'll be here," I said as I stood and shook his hand.

I was there on Friday, right on time. He came out of the back room to personally greet me and escorted me to his office.

"Isabel, I'm afraid I didn't find anything that fits your qualifications, but that's not to say something else won't come up in the next few days," he said.

I was very disappointed with the news but was secretly thrilled because it meant that I had not seen the last of him. We chatted for a while until we realized we were the last ones left in the office.

"Say, I haven't had anything to eat, and I'm starving. Would you like to join me for something to eat?" he asked.

"I know this really nice Dominican restaurant in my neighborhood that makes the best chicken stew."

"I'd love to," I said in my most controlled tone of voice. *Yes!*

He gave me a ride in his tiny standard-driven car to his Washington Heights neighborhood. I loved the way he expertly maneuvered the stick shift and the three foot pedals. Odd, I know, but there's something sexy about that, the way a man exudes power and control over what seems like a complicated operation without thinking about it.

He took me to a busy kitschy eatery with melted candles in empty sangria bottles on tables covered with plastic tablecloths and matching seat covers. Lively Spanish music played in the background.

We chose a cozy table for two near the picture window and continued our animated conversation while we waited for service. Eventually, a harried waiter came along and took our orders of stew with side salads and a bottle of red house wine.

We talked about our families, backgrounds, and interests. I learned that he was twenty-two, a Sagittarius, born in the Dominican Republic. He had just completed his bachelor's at John Jay College in psychology and wanted to work as a counselor for inner city teens. His anecdotes were full of funny stories about his family, which had me in stitches. I was in love by the time the stew came.

Frankie drove me home later that evening, gave me a gentlemanly kiss on the cheek, and promised to give me a call soon.

Needless to say, he never got me a job. I went back to the Soul and Latin Theater and was able to get my old job back working at public relations and doing some acting.

Frankie and I went out for dinner again, and on the third date, he took me to his bachelor pad, a two-room apartment on the upper west side. He popped open a bottle of red wine, put on his favorite romantic music, and continued to mesmerize me with his intellect and quick sense of humor. After a few glasses of wine, I was completely under his spell, allured by his charm and seductive magnetism.

He played one of my favorite salsa songs, "Anacaona" by Cheo Feliciano, written in tribute to a valiant Taina indian queen. I started to dance, moved by the resonant rhythm of the congas and the free-spirited spontaneity induced by the intoxicating wine. I was vaguely aware that he was watching me, and midway through the song, he joined me, swinging me to and fro until the song ended, and we fell laughing into each other's arms.

The next song was a slow romantic Harvey Averne ballad, and before I could sit down, he grabbed my arm and held me close as we swayed together to the sensuous mellifluous music. I laid my head on his muscular chest and he surrounded me with his strong arms in a firm embrace. By now, the full-bodied wine was making me feel uncomfortably lightheaded.

My mother's voice resounded in my head: "Never trust men. They're liars and are only after one thing. Never sit on a man's lap, and always keep your legs closed."

I've only known this guy for a short time. He's too charming. What if he's deliberately trying to seduce me? What if he put something in my drink...

"I'm sorry, Frankie, but it's getting late, and I need to leave." I felt embarrassed having to reveal that, although I was twenty, my mother would not allow me to date or bring men home.

"I'm disappointed, but I understand," he said.

I wasn't really sure if my mother would accept a visit from a boyfriend now that I was twenty and my younger sister was married. But I was certain that if I did tell her, she would be timing my dates and standing guard by the door like a watchdog waiting to pounce if I was a minute late. I decided not to say anything for now.

I asked Frankie to drop me off a block away in case Mother or one of her cronies was looking out the window.

Brunie, my best friend and now college roommate, still lived in El Barrio. As my confidante, she harbored my most intimate secrets. Overnight visits with her became my excuse to Mother whenever I wanted to spend some time with Frankie.

The fact that Mother insisted on having my friend's address and telephone number, like I was still a child, made me somewhat nervous, but I was confident that Brunie would know how to handle any unexpected awkward situations.

Frankie and I continued to see each other clandestinely, meeting in places where we would be unlikely to run into Mother or her informants.

I became dangerously obsessed with him. Conversation with him was effortless and stimulating. High-spirited moments brought laughter and joy. He became my world.

Once, after a wonderful night of dinner and dancing, we returned to Brunie's neighborhood. It was 3:00 a.m. and the street was deserted. Intoxicated with drink and the magic of the moment, we danced under the spotlight of a streetlamp as a light drizzle fell like stardust all around us. Frankie suddenly shouted, "Marry me, Isabel!" and without a second thought, I responded, "Yes, yes I will!"

I floated to Brunie's apartment and told her all about my amazing date and Frankie's proposal.

"Girl, I'm happy for you, but you don't know him long enough. Give yourself more time."

My day of departure arrived much too soon, but we had spent so much time together, that it seemed like we had known each other a lifetime.

Quite boldly, I informed Mother that a friend had offered to drive me to the airport and that he would be picking me up in a few minutes. I had forgotten that Mother had asked her stepsister and husband to drive me to the airport as well. She walked away silently.

When Frankie arrived to Mother's apartment, I introduced Frankie to her, but she coldly turned away without acknowledging him. Good Lord, had she found out about me and Frankie? What was going on here? I started to panic.

"Mami, *que te pasa*? What's wrong? You look angry."

"So *cabrona*! You bitch! What the hell is he doing here? Didn't I tell you that Cleo was taking you to the airport? Now I have to call her and tell her not to come. What an embarrassment! Go with him then, you whore, and don't you dare write to me or say anything because I don't want to know!" She quickly turned and walked away.

I could feel the heat of humiliation burning my face and the tears begin to sting as I turned to look at Frankie, who was sitting in a chair looking dumbfounded. I was speechless, feeling completely disgraced and shocked by my mother's unwarranted outburst. This was not the send-off I expected nor the person I wanted Frankie to know.

"I think you should leave her alone for now and let's just go," said Frankie.

"Right," I said softly, and with tears flowing, I said good-bye to Grandma, who whispered in my ear, "Try and find it in your heart to forgive her."

I hugged my brothers and little Bernie, and as I clung to them, I promised I would bring something nice for them when I got back.

Frankie and I rode silently to the airport.

"Your mother has quite a temper, doesn't she?" he finally said.

"Yes, she does," I replied as I dabbed at my eyes with a soaked tissue. "I am so sorry this had to happen."

"Oh no, don't mind me. I feel bad for *you*. Give her a little time. She'll get over it," he said. "Keep your mind on the fantastic adventure that's ahead of you. It's going to be great." After a pause, "I wish I was going with you."

"I wish you were too," I said as I made a losing effort to stop myself from crying again. "I'm going to miss you so much."

"Ah, come on, mi Anacaona," he said as he playfully ruffled my hair. "I'm going to miss you too, but you know I'll write to you often, and you can always call me collect if it gets rough for you."

I was in deep thought as we made our way through the South Bronx and onto the Major Deegan Expressway into Queens. Frankie put on some upbeat salsa music and made corny jokes about the French, trying to cheer me up. Before long, he had me laughing until my sides hurt.

Arriving at the airport's parking lot, the mood became somber once again as I was forced to confront the moment I had been dreading. I didn't want to look at him, didn't want him touching me, didn't want to say good-bye.

Fate was on my side for as we entered the main terminal, there stood Professor Bartow, who announced that it was getting late and I needed to hurry. As my mentor grabbed my bags, I had but seconds to quickly embrace the love of my life, my tears flowing onto his cheeks as we kissed good-bye.

"No, it's not good-bye, Isabel. It's see you soon, mi Anacaona," he said.

The group boarded a bus that would transport us to the Air France gate, and as it took off from the main terminal, I looked out the window hoping to catch a final glimpse of Frankie, but he was gone.

Within what seemed like fleeting hours through time and space, I went from the streets of the South Bronx to Paris, France. The moment we disembarked, my group's lively chatter ceased as we slowly absorbed the hectic milieu at the main terminal in an awe-struck trance. We were ushered through customs and baggage claims, then onto a bus that took us to the hostel located in the Latin Quarter section of Paris.

The dramatic change in scenery revived me as I peered past the filmy window at the passing images. The pages of my travel books had come to life, and somehow I had become a part of the descriptive prose. I thought, any minute now, I'm going to wake up.

We traveled through highways with French signs and billboards and into the traffic-jammed city with its provincial architecture and tree-lined boulevards. It was all so different, so surreal and so new. My senses went into a hypnotic meltdown as jet lag and the excitement of being there, of seeing all the streets and monuments I'd read about so many times finally became real. Alice had arrived in wonderland!

We disembarked in front of an antiquated hostel where we were assigned our double-bedded rooms. Debbie and I decided to find somewhere to eat as the hunger pangs took precedence over our exhaustion. Making sure not to veer too far off lest we get lost, we walked a straight path from the hostel, searching for an eatery.

We finally came upon a small café that advertised a food item we recognized: "Sandwiche" it said on a cardboard poster in the window. Timidly and in our best French, we ordered half a baguette each with ham and cheese and a soda.

It was nightfall by the time we wearily made our way back to the hotel, mighty pleased with ourselves after having ordered our first meal in French and being understood.

For the next three weeks, we attended classes at a small school within walking distance from the hostel. After class, a group of us would get a sandwiche and drinks and we'd picnic in the beautiful Jardin du Luxembourg gardens.

I quickly learned to navigate the metro and visited the Louvre museum and the Arc de Triomphe. I climbed the steep steps to the exquisite Sacré Coeur church and observed artists create stunning portraits in Montmartre. I walked down the Champs Élysées Boulevard with its ritzy shops and swanky restaurants and had cheese and wine on the grassy knolls beneath the daunting Eiffel Tower.

Someone in our group took a photo of me standing on a parapet in front of the beautiful fountains facing the Tower. That photo became a precious keepsake for it captured forever a split second in time that would never repeat itself.

Since then, I have kept a special box where I keep all of my treasured photographs. Those static images have the uncanny ability to jar the memory and bring places and people back to life. They bridge the present with the past and validate as real what the passage of time has turned into hazy recollections. Were it not for them, my experiences would have remained as just imperfect memories of perfect moments.

On a Saturday night, a group of us went out for a meal and drinks. After a few bottles of wine, we took a walk along the spellbinding Seine River. The moon's reflection shone brilliantly against the still waters under a vast canopy of flickering stars. I could easily see why this was considered a landmark for lovers.

Although it was late by the time we got back to the hostel, we were still feeling quite tipsy and silly. One of the guys had brought along his tape player, and he set it down in the middle of a cobblestone alleyway. "Dancing in the Street" by Martha Reeves and the Vandellas boomed from its solid speakers, and we all started dancing and singing at the top of our lungs until people began shouting out their windows for us to stop.

I was glad that my studies and my new friends kept me busy for it was in the quiet moments that I missed Frankie the most. He had given me a tape with our favorite music, which I listened to while writing him postcards and letters or gazing at his reflection in my bedroom window.

I had phoned Frankie two days after I arrived, and he was so surprised and happy to hear from me. Listening to his voice made him feel that much closer, and that night, I dreamed of being with him again and planning our future together.

Our orientation period in Paris came to an end, and once again we boarded a bus which took us to Rouen. Debbie and I were, in fact, placed with an older couple, and admittedly, I was nervous about meeting them and what to say.

On our arrival, there were several families waiting but we recognized ours immediately. The couple appeared to be in their late sixties. Monsieur Marfil was a rotund gentleman with wisps of white hair barely visible on his shiny pate and pinched-red cheeks. Blue suspenders stretched across his rotund belly under a worn cardigan that had seen better days.

Madame Marfil was a petite, matronly woman whose tinted dark brown hair was loosely piled into a bun. Large glasses overwhelmed her gaunt face, but her bright eyes and warm smile made me think of my grandma, and I felt an instant connection to her.

It was now sink or swim for neither one of our host parents spoke a word of English.

"*Ça va?*" I said to Monsieur Marfil as I shook his hand. He started to laugh. I have no idea what made me say that. Ça va in French is equivalent to "how's it going," which was a dumb thing to say, but it broke the ice. From then on, he and I hit it off splendidly.

Monsieur and Madame Marfil lived in a large but humble two-story home up a steep cobblestoned street. They showed Debbie and me to our room on the second floor. It had two twin beds covered with thick flowered comforters, two small desks for studying, and two large armoires. I chose the desk facing a tall French window that overlooked the front courtyard.

Downstairs was the dining area with a six-seat table, a small den just off the dining room where Monsieur Marfil did his paperwork, and a large, warm kitchen. The home was modestly decorated with worn antique furnishings, but I loved its simplicity and old-fashioned charm.

It was in her quaint kitchen where Maman Marfil taught me how to cook French dishes on her antiquated coal-burning stove. Sometimes when I got home from school, she'd send me off to the corner store to buy baguettes and yoghurt for dessert. Later, while preparing dinner, we'd exchange stories about her life or my family back home.

We always ate dinner together, which was an unfamiliar practice for me. For a starter, we would have a bowlful of delicious creamy potato or broccoli soup, then roast chicken and parslied potatoes with corn or boiled carrots. For dessert, we'd have yoghurt or a slice of home-made sponge cake and a huge cup of coffee served in a small bowl rather than a cup.

All through dinner, we would converse with Maman and Papa mostly about school, though I would often ask them questions about their lives and growing up in France. They didn't have a clue what a Puerto Rican was, so I showed them where it was on a map and told them all about the island and our culture.

My greatest challenge became dragging myself from underneath the warm covers to go to the bathroom in the middle of the night, especially when it was cold outside as the toilet was in an outhouse.

For a bath, we had to first turn on the water heater in the kitchen, then go outdoors to a small wooden shed where we had to stand in a large tin barrel and shower with a hand-held sprayer. It was murder when the weather turned cold as there was no heat in the shed. Having lived in places where we were often deprived of heat in the winter and where the use of the bathtub in the kitchen was limited, I didn't mind the inconvenience.

Not long after I arrived in Rouen, I sent my mother a postcard.

Dear Mami,

I am so sorry for our misunderstanding. I hope that you accept my apology and that we can put this incident behind us. I do love and miss you and I can't imagine that you would not speak to me again over something so insignificant. Please think about it as I would like to go home and be a family again. I love you very much, Isabel.

Several postcards later, I received a letter from her in which she told me all about the folks back home but never referred to the incident again.

Rouen is the capital of Normandy, a historic region near the northern coast of France. Heavily damaged during WWII, Rouen has maintained its old-world charm with its surviving half-timbered buildings, archaic Gothic architecture, and narrow cobblestone streets.

The busiest street in Rouen is the Place du Vieux Marché. Along with scores of small shops and sidewalk cafes, it features the Gros Horloge, an astronomical clock built in the 14th century which sits atop a stone arch that spans the width of the narrow walkway. The intricate details that embellish the clock and its archway are breathtaking. Every hour, the clock strikes with a resounding bong that can be heard throughout the city.

Joan of Arc was burned at the stake in Rouen in 1431, and at the time I was there, a magnificent statue of Joan on her horse marked the spot where she died. It was eerie yet humbling to stand on the same spot where a historic figure of such magnitude had once been. Since then, a modern church in the shape of a funeral pyre has been built in Joan's honor on the site of her execution.

For winter break, a group of us decided to visit London. We traveled to the northern port city of Calais in France where we embarked on a boat that sailed across the English Channel to Dover, England. As we crossed the choppy channel escorted by a noisy flock of seagulls, I could see the famous white cliffs of Dover in the hazy distance, rising from the waters along the English coastline like giant icebergs.

I had never been on a boat, and it was actually great fun trying to keep our balance as it swayed side-to-side, but after a while, the awful queasiness began to set in and took the wind out of our sails.

London was colorful and exciting, and what was really neat was that everyone spoke like the Beatles. I loved Piccadilly Circus, an area that reminded me of Times Square with its rolling marquees, trendy shops, theaters, and crowded streets. We visited Madame Tussaud's Wax Museum with its eerie life-like figures of famous personalities and watched the changing of the guard at Buckingham Palace.

I ventured out alone one day and strolled through Carnaby Street, an area once known as a gathering place for hippies and still popular among the outlandish for their mod clothes and accessories. I couldn't help myself and splurged on a pair of retro pleated pants and cool platform shoes.

Mounting a bright red double-decker bus at the end of the day, I sat on the open-air top level and enjoyed the shifting scenery as the wind played havoc with my hair.

Mercurial and manic, London was a whirlwind love affair that immersed me in all its decadent flamboyance and regal pageantry. And like a tempestuous lover whose taste leaves you yearning for more, I vowed that I would someday return. I was very disappointed that I had come this far and didn't get a chance to visit Liverpool, the birthplace of my childhood idols. But who knew what the future would bring.

My stay in France came to a bittersweet end for although I was glad to be headed home to see Frankie and my friends and family, I had to say good-by to my dear, sweet French parents. Before Papa Marfil drove me to the train station, he had a quiet word with me in the dining room.

"We have a custom in France that when good friends depart, we give them a pocketknife as a symbolic gesture to remind them that the threads that bind us in friendship shall never be severed." He held open my hand and placed a small red pocketknife in my palm and closed my fingers around it. "Madame Marfil and I have thoroughly enjoyed having you with us, and we hope that you will keep in touch with us, as in the short time we have known you, we have come to appreciate you like a daughter." I was so touched by his gesture for I had never heard such kind words spoken with more sincerity or meaning.

I hugged Maman and couldn't let go until Papa announced it was time to leave. I said so long to my roommate Debbie, who had decided to stay the summer with some of the gang and traipse around Europe, lucky them.

At the train station, I hugged Papa once again, and all I can remember saying over and over again was, "Thank you, thank you so much!"

I kept my promise, and over the years, I continued to write to Maman, who was the letter writer in the family. We communicated frequently until one day she wrote that Papa had fallen and broken his hip, and he was now in a nursing home because she could no longer care for him. She moved to a small apartment near him, and after that, I never heard from her again.

I have never forgotten them and oftentimes read her letters, which I have kept as remembrances of kindred spirits halfway across the world who once embraced me as one of their own.

It was a long, lonely plane ride back to the states and lonelier still when I arrived, for there was no one at the airport to meet me. I took a taxi back to the South Bronx, and as I rode past the familiar roadways and landmarks, I felt like I had never left. Digging into my jeans' pocket, I took out the little pocket knife that Papa had given me and fingered it all the way home.

"Hola, Mami!" I said as I enthusiastically hugged her when she opened the door. "How have you been?"

"Good," she said. "The usual aches and pains but nothing serious. How was your flight?"

"Long and boring." I followed her into the kitchen where she continued to stir a casserole. "So where is everybody? Where is Grandma?" I asked her.

"Grandma went to the doctor this morning and she's still not back. Gil is downstairs, and Edwin and your little sister are watching TV in their rooms."

"Okay." I picked up my suitcases and went to greet my siblings. They were thrilled with the little trinkets I had bought them. Later I called Frankie and left a message on his answering machine to let him know that I was home.

That summer, Frankie and I saw each other every chance we got and had a glorious time no matter where we went or what we did.

One evening, I made plans to go out dancing with Frankie and spend the night at his place while giving Mother the usual story that I was staying overnight at Brunie's house.

I got all dolled up and headed out to my friend's place to wait for Frankie. Nine o'clock, ten o'clock and no word from Frankie. There was no answer when I phoned him. I started to worry as I hung out Brunie's window, hoping to catch a glimpse of his car. Eleven o'clock, midnight, still no Frankie. It was one o'clock in the morning, and I still half expected him to show.

Suddenly, through the half open window, I heard my name being called from the street below.

"Jesus, Brunie, that sounds like my mother!"

"It can't be," she said as we both ran to the window and looked out. Sure enough, there was my mother standing on the street below.

"What is she doing here at this hour? How did she get here from the Bronx?" Brunie asked me, like I had the answers to my mother's weird tactics.

"I don't know, Brunie! What should I do now?" Silly me, I was where I was supposed to be. Not having anything to hide except for the sexy dress I was wearing at this ungodly hour, I quickly stripped, put on my pajamas and Brunie's bathrobe, and ran downstairs as quickly as my heels could carry me. *Oh no, my heels!* I took off my stilettos and left them on the bottom steps and continued barefoot to the sidewalk where my mother was standing.

"Mami, what are you doing here? What's happened?" I asked her.

"I just came from playing loteria at Gloria's house and stopped by to make sure that this is where you were. Make sure you get home early as I have a lot of errands to run, and I'm going to need your help," she said. It was an unlikely excuse, but I was relieved that she had found me where she expected me to be.

"Okay, Mami. I'll be home early." I watched her jump into a waiting car and breathed a sigh of relief.

The next afternoon, I finally managed to get a hold of Frankie, who apologetically explained that he had spent the early evening at his brother's house and had gotten drunk and passed out. He made up for it the next evening with a movie, dinner, and drinks at his place complemented by a lot of laughter and whispered sweet nothings. Needless to say, my anger was very short-lived.

I returned to UConn in the fall, but instead of staying in a dorm, Brunie and I decided to share an off-campus apartment. We hitched rides to school and back, a practice that was widespread in those days. First chance I got, I headed back to New York to spend a relaxing weekend with Frankie.

That particular Saturday, Frankie had to go to work, and I decided to make myself useful by cleaning his apartment and preparing a nice dinner for us. With plenty of time on my hands before his arrival, I decided to do his laundry.

There among his personal items was a flimsy night-gown... and it wasn't mine.

The shock numbed my senses. I couldn't feel, couldn't move, couldn't think straight.

I don't know how long I sat there in suspended disbelief, but the next thing I knew, his keys were jangling at the door. I quickly shoved the gown underneath the sofa cushion just in time for Frankie to appear at the doorway with that wicked smile that had stolen my heart so long ago. I stoically pretended like nothing happened while I mentally prepared myself to hear what I didn't want to know.

"Boy, that sure smells good! What's cooking?" he asked as he gave me a peck on the lips.

"London broil," I said, trying to sound nonchalant.

He went on ranting about his dreadful day at work while I continued to find enough strength to confront him and face whatever excuse he dished out. In spite of the obvious, I wanted to give him the benefit of the doubt.

He finally sat down next to me on the sofa. "What's wrong? Are you okay?" he asked with great concern.

I slipped my hand under the cushion and brought out the nightgown. "Frankie, I found this in your laundry. Can you tell me what this is all about?" My heart began to race as I waited for an answer.

His face visibly paled, then turned into a pensive frown. "I'm trying to think," he said. "I believe my sister left it here when she stayed over the day before we went to the beach."

"Frankie, I wasn't born yesterday. What's going on? Whose gown is this?" I tried to appear as unemotional as possible so he wouldn't see the pain in my eyes.

After a long pause, he took a deep breath. "I didn't know how to tell you without hurting you. I guess this is as good a time as any. Isabel... I've been seeing someone else. I'm so sorry. I love you both and believe me, this has been very hard on me..."

"How long has this been going on, Frankie?"

"I met her just after I met you." He looked straight into my eyes as he spoke.

"You mean to tell me that you've been seeing her all the time you've been with me?"

"Yes," he said.

I didn't want to hear anymore. Every time he spoke, he drove that knife deeper into my heart. I could feel an agonizing scream building up inside, like a wounded animal in the throes of death.

Seeing no emotion on my part, he continued to cleanse his conscience while destroying my soul. "I'm in love with both of you but for different reasons. I knew that eventually I would have to make a choice, but I kept putting it off because I didn't want to hurt either of you. Before I knew it, she was talking marriage and making plans, and I just went with it. I've always thought of you as the stronger one..."

"Why, Frankie? Why her and not me!"

"Honestly, Isabel, because I can fool her but I could never fool you."

"You can't have both of us, Frankie. It's either her or me." After a pause, "How serious is this?" I asked, barely able to get the words out.

"We're planning to get married in April."

I had tried everything in my power to maintain some semblance of dignity and self-control, but the final blow was too much to bear. I cried uncontrollably while he held me and rocked me until eventually I fell asleep.

He continued to tell me that he loved us both and I, unable to let go, foolishly stood by while he moved forward with his wedding plans. Whatever his motivation, he freely shared with me the details of his upcoming nuptials, and I pretended to be happy for him, unshaken by the fact that he was having his cake and eating it too. I went into complete denial, believing that if I remained persistent, I could win him back.

To any rational, objective outsider with an iota of self-respect, this scenario would have been unfathomable, unacceptable; but to me, incapable of being impartial, completely engrossed in this man whom I loved more than I obviously loved myself, this became a challenge that I just had to overcome.

In retrospect, my actions begged the question: Was it really love that drove me? What was there to love about a man who had so coldheartedly betrayed me?

One early Saturday morning, I was in Frankie's apartment when the doorbell rang from downstairs. We looked at each other wide-eyed.

"Who is it?" he asked through the intercom.

"It's me, Aida!" answered the tinny voice.

"Oh shit, it's her!" he said to me with panic in his voice. For some stupid reason, I started to panic too. "Wait here while I go downstairs and find out what she wants," he said. No sooner had he finished throwing on a shirt and dungarees, there was a knock on the door.

"Dammit, she's at the door!" he said. "Quick, get in the closet."

I crouched in the middle of a pile of linen and boxes on the floor of his tiny closet and covered myself loosely with a blanket as he shut the closet door.

I heard him greet Aida and two other females who had accompanied her. For whatever reason, Frankie left momentarily with Aida, leaving the two females to wait in the apartment. Suddenly, their voices sounded closer as they entered the room where I was secluded.

"I wonder if he's hiding something," I heard one say as she opened the closet door. I held my breath under the blanket, frozen in place. "Man, he's got a lot of junk here," she said, and with a sudden move, she kicked the blanket, missing my legs by inches.

"Hey! What're you doing in my closet?" I heard Frankie yell. Soon as the closet door closed, I began to slowly expel air from my heaving lungs.

The second I heard them all leave, I got dressed and out of there while I still had my life in my hands. The whole ordeal seemed ridiculous in hindsight, for I should have let them find me and blown his perfect threesome to hell. But the stark reality was that I was now, in fact, the other woman.

I returned to my lonely apartment in Connecticut and agonized over my lost love. I made earnest attempts to stop seeing and calling him, but like an addiction, my weakness and vulnerability made it too hard to distance myself, and I was soon back on the phone with him. In turn, he made feeble efforts to stop me from contacting him but, then again, he wanted us both, didn't he? I continued to call Frankie and visit him in New York, clinging to the delusive hope that he would have a change of heart.

One day, while staring in the mirror at the reflection of a woman I no longer knew, I discovered a large bald spot on my scalp. Within a few weeks, I had lost patches of hair all over my head. I went around wearing a bandanna until I was able to afford a skin specialist, who gave me shots in my scalp to make my hair grow back.

Unable to endure my capricious bawling and bouts of ambiguous silence, Brunie moved out of the apartment. Frankly, I couldn't blame her. I was forced to vacate the apartment and stayed wherever anyone would have me.

But no matter what, I owed it to myself to finish what I had started out to do, and in June, 1974, I completed my degree, majoring in sociology with a minor in French. With that, I hoped to get into hospital management, and I set that as my new goal.

The point of no return in Frankie's wedding plans became evident. The heartbreaking reality that he was going to go through with the marriage and the futility of my efforts began to finally sink in.

I thought I was going to lose my mind. I can only liken the experience to a junkie's pain of withdrawal in ridding myself of this toxic obsession. Somehow I made it through his wedding date, and that's all I could hope for, to make it through one day at a time.

It would have been easy for me to crawl into a dark hole and waste my life thinking about what could have been, what I had done wrong, what I could have done differently. The easy thing to do would have been to appease him and continue to be the other woman at the expense of my self-respect and dignity.

I found that by surrounding myself with good friends who understood and pushing myself to go out socially provided the diversion I needed to finally get over missing him. In time, I emerged that much stronger but more cynical and impervious as I came to realize that I wasn't the only one who had known betrayal.

I immersed myself in self-help books and learned that I needed to stop analyzing his actions and focus on my role in this ordeal as a way of helping myself regain what I had lost. Unfortunately for him, I missed the chapter on how to deal with the residual anger that cropped up when I finally stripped him of the false illusion I had created and saw him in the light of truth. I was angry, and I knew of only one way to rid myself of the rage.

Nearly a year after his nuptials, I called him up out of the blue and invited him to come over, and he was only too happy to oblige. By this time, I had moved into my own place, a nice one-bedroom apartment in the Bronx.

His appearance was shocking. Having immersed himself in the security and languid comfort of marital bliss, he had gained weight and appeared at my door after work in his business attire with sweaty armpits and overhanging belly. The only recognizable features were his voice and gleaming smile.

I had no animosity towards his wife, but I wanted her to know that he thought he could fool her but not me. Just before he arrived, I sprayed myself with perfume, which I hate. I rubbed myself all over him but refused to have sex with the two-timing ogre and sent him on his way home.

He called me the next day and told me that his wife became furious when she smelled the perfume on him, but he managed to get out of it by telling her that his client's perfumed pooch had climbed all over him. I'd overlooked what a cunning liar he was.

On another occasion, I enticed him to spend a weekend with me. He told his wife he had to go on a business trip, packed his bag, and came over. When he came, I was gone. I never found out how he got out of that one.

I never saw him again.

Getting my own place was liberating and exciting. I could come and go as I pleased with whomever I wanted or just stay home in my own space and relax. In my quiet times, I enjoyed listening to my massive collection of Latin and R&B music or reading a good book. I loved to go out dancing to salsa clubs, which I did every chance I got. That's how I got fired from my first job.

Right after college, I went to work for a Cuban female doctor in the lower east side. A couple of times, I showed up to work after only a few hours of sleep and the funk of rum and cokes emanating from my pores. It was either that or the time she was attempting to show me how to give an injection to an unsuspecting patient that got me the boot.

I was ready to squeamishly plunge the needle into the poor lady's massive buttock when the doctor suddenly exclaimed, "Oh look, *un bicho*," as she swatted a fly. I went into a fit of hysterical laughter, and the doctor had to give the shot herself. Apparently, Cubans use the same word for a fly as Puerto Ricans use for penis, a fact I wasn't aware of until that day.

My first real job was working at Greenpoint Hospital in Brooklyn as assistant manager of the outpatient clinics. My immediate supervisor was an elderly Phyllis Diller look-alike who smoked like a chimney and was always adjusting her curly wig. She had a great sense of humor and infused a lighthearted mood to a very stressful setting.

As my capabilities became more apparent, she began to unload greater responsibilities on me while spending more time in our tiny shared office in a cloud of smoke. In spite of my youth (I was only twenty-two), I was able to manage a much older staff, although dealing with union reps was a particularly unique challenge.

Enter Twanda, a heavy-set mound of mocha lard with a badass 'tude who could put the fear of God in anybody just by showing up. One could never underestimate Twanda's ghetto toughness and hoochie image for she was highly intelligent and knew that union codebook by heart. A minor union infraction against an employee would have Twanda's wrath at my office door in no time, with good old Phyllis making a hasty exit the minute she heard the Amazon viper was on her way.

But life was good. I was working, had my own space, had my small circle of friends, and was actively dating.

At Greenpoint, I met a chocolate bonbon named Warrell who was a counselor in the substance abuse clinic. Tall, slim, and gorgeous, he looked like a GQ model whose confident appearance veiled a soft and sweet persona. To my amazement, he turned out to be one of the greatest salsa partners I had ever danced with, and I showed him off like a trophy every chance I got.

Unfortunately, Warrell was more into me than I was into him, and his clinginess eventually began to irritate me. One evening, he called me and began to tell me a sordid tale of woe.

"Isabel, you're not going to believe this. I just got home and there was an eviction notice under my door. I don't know what to do!" he griped with rapid-fire speech.

"Well, Warrell, do you owe the money or is it a mistake?" I asked, hoping the serenity in my voice would calm him down.

"No...I don't know! I thought my ex had paid, but now I don't know!" My calm approach was not working. He was getting more flustered.

"Warrell, try to relax and think. Do you have any rent receipts around the house? Can you call your ex and ask her if she paid the rent?" This is not normal, I thought.

"I don't know how to contact her! What am I going to do? What if they throw me out?" He started to cry.

I made up my mind. Warrell had to go, but how to tell him? Definitely now was not a good time.

"Warrell, go through your drawers tonight and look for receipts. If you don't find any, call your landlord in the morning and tell him your situation. I'm sure they'll work something out with you."

"You really think they'll do that?" The crying turned to sniffles. It was starting to work.

"Yes, I really do. Now go have a drink of wine and go to sleep. You'll be able to think much clearer in the morning."

"Oh God, I feel a little better now. Thanks, Isabel. Can I call you tomorrow?"

"Sure, Warrell, sure."

A few days later, when the storm had passed, he called to ask me out.

"I'm sorry, Warrell, but I don't think we should take this any further. You're a wonderful guy, but I'm not ready to be in a steady relationship with anyone."

"Why, Isabel? Is it something I said or did?"

"No, Warrell. It's not you, it's me." I can't believe I said that, but the deed was done. It was over.

In a short period of time, I assembled a small posse of single Latina vixens who lived to hustle (as in the dance) and could slip into their swirling rayon hoochie dresses and platforms in a New York minute. Our favorite nightspots were the Chez Jose, Broadway Casino, El Hipocampo, and Casablanca, with the Corso topping the A-list.

It was at one of these stomping grounds that I reunited with my childhood friend, Maria, who quickly became my number one fly girl amongst my sisterhood of disco divas. She introduced me to the Epoca Club in the Bronx, which was conveniently located a short distance from where she lived. Maria was a brilliant dancer and knew how to lead better than the most agile male partner. So when there were no male volunteers, she and I would tear up the dance floor like we owned it. A great time was a given when the mambo queen was in the house.

Maria's sassiness and bravura were not innate gifts but the acquired aftereffects of a painful childhood that she'd say she would rather forget. She was raised by older sisters who were barely past adolescence themselves. After their mother died during childbirth, their neglectful father left them to their own devices.

She once told me that he would visit briefly and leave money for rent and food and scars from whippings, as if the punishment he inflicted could relieve him of the anger he felt for a responsibility he didn't want.

Like many of us, she grew up dirt poor and carried demoralizing secrets beneath a split veneer of girlish exuberance and tough street smarts. Maria's goals were not to reach academic summits but just to survive.

When I met Maria again, she was working, sharing a nice apartment in a private house, hanging out with friends, and agonizing over a man. She had been seeing some player who was carrying on "exclusive" relationships with multiple girls simultaneously. Casanova Brown had been snagged with some bimho but, being a player, he knew exactly how to keep them both gaga and weak-kneed.

Even savvy girls can fall prey to smooth talking guys who know how to target our G-spots. That guy took her heart, melted it, molded it to suit him, then broke it and handed it back to her in a million pieces for her to mend on her own. But being a survivor, Maria stoically feigned indifference while privately enduring the heartbreak of dismantling the dreams she had built around him.

Then there was Olga, a pixie cherub with big hazel eyes whose mission in life was to find Mr. Right. Olga was a talented textile designer who lived in an artistically decorated walk-in closet on Manhattan's upper west side, conveniently located near our midtown hangouts.

Although a very attractive girl, she was a bit ditzy with a Teflon brain—nothing stuck with her. Olga was the sort who thought Latin was spoken in Rome or who might soberly inquire how to spell IOU, bless her.

But she was a loyal friend without a mean bone in her body and always up for a good time on the town. Unfortunately, her gullibility and sweetness caused her to gravitate towards smooth-talking reprobates who sucked the life out of her, leaving her wondering afterwards why she felt like a dry prune.

Having freed myself from the users and the useless, I now felt a palpable joie de vivre that shined through my persona and became a magnet for those looking to associate with someone carefree and seemingly secure in her own skin.

One evening, I was sitting at a table with Olga and Maria at the Chez Jose, downing rum and cokes while grooving to the music and having a good laugh. When the next song started, I felt a finger tapping my shoulder.

Beside me stood an extraordinary piece of Michelangelo art in human form. His face was unblemished porcelain and his ocean-blue eyes sparkled like starry reflections on a calm sea. He was decked out in a suit and open shirt, his jet black hair neatly combed in a DA style. His welcoming smile revealed perfect pearl-white teeth complemented by a pair of full seductive lips. I was in love again.

We danced the rest of the night, his perfumed aroma arousing my sensual cravings and suppressing my inhibitions, and when we danced to a slow bolero, all sorts of lecherous thoughts ran through my head.

Richie called me the following day and asked if I would like to accompany him to his co-worker's home for dinner that evening, an offer I readily accepted. We held hands in the cab all the way to his friend's house as we chatted about our lives, likes, and dislikes. It was uncanny how much we had in common.

We had a lovely meal at his friend Benny's apartment, followed by several glasses of fine wine. At just the right moment, Benny played "The Way We Were" by Barbra Streisand. Richie impulsively took my hand and enclosed me in his arms. We began to dance as Barbra's dulcet voice serenaded us. The same song played over and over until we realized that Benny was no longer in the room. That's when he kissed me—soft, sweet, perfect.

Those lascivious thoughts came rushing back, and he must have felt the same, for we abruptly separated, hastily thanked Benny for his hospitality, and made a quick getaway back to my apartment.

"Oh my God," exclaimed Olga the next day, her eyes wide with shock. "He could have been a serial killer, for all you know."

"No, Olga, highly unlikely. If he was a murderer, he wouldn't have taken me to his co-worker's apartment, don't you think?"

"I guess," she said, still unsure.

"So how was it?" asked Janet, the newest addition to my jalapeño posse.

Janet was a seductive temptress I had met through Olga who had no problem taking her pick from the scores of suitors who were captivated by the mere swish of her hair. We could have hated her but she became a loyal friend who respected our love interests with nary a batted eyelash directed their way. She knew better.

"Janet, I wish I could tell you it was heavenly, but the truth of the matter is he had a hard time." They giggled, a reaction that went right over my head. Olga looked confused.

"The gun melted and the bullet never discharged," Janet clarified.

It took a moment for the penny to drop with Olga. "You don't say!"

"What a shame," said Janet. "Are you going to see him again?"

"Sure I'll see him again. He's a really nice guy and even nicer to look at. Maybe it was just a one-off thing."

But it wasn't.

Richie worked the evening shift, and I sometimes found myself preparing a sumptuous dinner for him at all kinds of late hours. He was a wonderful conversationalist with a great sense of humor and worthy of my patient understanding with his shortcomings. I thought this was something we could work with, but he soon began making excuses for not staying after a visit. Once, he even brought an unexpected friend for dinner, and it was clear to me why.

Eventually Richie started becoming more detached until he finally revealed one day that he wanted to date other women as well and that he was, in fact, seeing another girl.

"How very convenient," I said to him.

"Well, I've got the best of both worlds. She's a great housekeeper and you're a great cook," he said, baring his pearly whites with a childish giggle.

Déjà vu hit me like a ton of bricks. I should have smacked that grin right off his face as Mother would have done. Instead, I started dating other men as well while keeping Richie as a friend, always hoping that he'd grow up and come to his senses. When he did, it was too late.

Richie surprised me one evening by taking the initiative to call and invite himself over for a midnight meal, but by this time, my future husband had come into my life.

"I'm sorry, Richie, but you can't come over. Not tonight and not ever. I'm engaged now. and my fiancé is here."

"Wow that was quick. Well, congratulations, then. I wish you the best," he said sullenly.

A year or two later, I saw Richie on the subway platform. He passed right by me, looked right through me, and pretended he didn't even know me.

That Christmas, I met with my old UConn chum, Norma, who had married her college sweetheart, Luis, and was preparing to take a belated honeymoon trip with him to

Puerto Rico. I mentioned to her that I had been meaning to visit my sister and her new husband in Naranjito, and they kindly offered to let me tag along.

We spent a few relaxing days visiting with Luis's mother, then took several beat-up taxis and rickety buses through enchanting picturesque towns, staying overnight wherever there were relatives who would have us.

Puerto Rico's rich natural beauty is graciously complemented by the warm hospitality of its people, a custom that extends beyond close relatives to include friends and even strangers. It's not unheard of to appear unexpectedly at a relative's doorstep and be received with open arms, given a warm meal and a place to rest, no matter what sleeping arrangements needed to be invented.

At one of our stops, it wasn't until the bus had left in a cloud of exhaust smoke that I realized my suitcase was still on it. Luis's aunt, who wasn't expecting us, gathered some basic attire and toiletries for me until I could get to a larger town with a mall or department store. I was humbled by the kindness of this woman I didn't even know.

The next evening, well-rested, fed, and with less baggage, we traveled down dark countrysides and up narrow mountain roads towards Naranjito. Looking down into the valley, it seemed like the sky and earth had exchanged places, with the lights of tiny hamlets along the slopes glimmering like stars. I could smell the freshness of the earth and hear the distinct mating sounds of the coquis as they sang in their cacophonous choir.

Soon we found ourselves in the tiny town that my sister now called home. We got off the bus and began to walk up a dark dirt road. Along the sides were shacks and cement houses with flickering holiday lights and music blaring from the open doorways. The dismal conditions did not seem to dampen people's spirits as the merriment took to the streets and balconies.

As we trekked further up the hill, we came upon a group of merrymakers gaily singing traditional Christmas songs in front of a humbly decorated wooden house.

I carefully scanned the crowd, looking for that familiar face, the search made more difficult by the darkness and its deceptive shadows. Suddenly...

"Wanda! Wanda!" She turned and looked at me with disbelief. I ran to her, arms outstretched, as she rushed to meet me. We hugged endlessly and cried. I had missed her so much!

"Oh, Isabel, I can't believe you're here!"

"I can't believe I'm here either!"

I hugged Sammy and quickly introduced them to my friends. We held on to each other all night long as we joined the crowd on their stops to various homes, each resident welcoming the revelers with drinks and tasty holiday treats. The fiesta carried on until the break of dawn.

As my friends napped early that morning, my sister and I chatted over a strong cup of coffee. "Tell me, Wanda, are you happy here?"

"Oh, Isabel, I love it here! We all know each other and my neighbors are so sweet. And look at this view," she said as she extended her arm, pointing to the beauty of the valley behind her modest home. "Not to mention the beautiful weather here. Being high up in the mountains, I get a nice breeze even on the hottest days."

"What about Sammy? Is he being good to you? Is he behaving himself?"

She blushed as she answered, "Isabel, he is very good to me. He cleans, he cooks, not at all like most men around here who wouldn't lift a spoon or a broom to help out. And his family is very good to me too."

"But Wanda, don't you miss New York? Life here is so different."

"I miss New York a little, but I miss the family more. I don't miss the weather, though. Here you can leave your living room and go out on the balcony with a cup of coffee and just enjoy the scenery or talk with the neighbors whenever you want. You can't do that in New York," she said, taking a swig of her coffee.

"I guess you're right. I just want to know that you're happy, and you seem to be."

"I am, Isabel. I'm very happy."

My sister had always had a knack for looking at the bright side of things, always cheerful and never complaining. I was convinced that she meant it when she said that she was happy, and I felt better about leaving her behind.

Sammy dropped us off at a remote bus stop that afternoon. While waiting for the bus, I began to look around and noticed a group of friends playing basketball on a dirt court across the road. There was something vaguely familiar about one of the guys in the group. I honed in on him, trying for the life of me to remember where I had seen him.

It hit me like a swat on a fly. It was Rico, the troglodyte I had gifted with my chastity back at Harvard.

"You see that guy over there with the curly hair and green t-shirt?" I whispered to Norma and Luis. "I know him. I went out with him a long time ago."

"Really!" said Norma.

"Why don't you say hello?" prompted Luis.

"I don't want to," I said. "He probably won't even remember me."

"Give it a shot. Call him over. You want me to call him for you?" offered Luis.

"No, I don't think so."

"What's his name?"

"His name is Rico. But Luis, I don't..."

"Hey, Rico! *Oye Rico, ven aqui!*" Luis called out to him.

I looked around for someplace to bury my head as Rico began to cross the road.

"Noooooo!" said Olga with her signature wide-eyed expression as I recounted my latest adventure. "Did he recognize you?"

"At first he didn't, but I just stood there and smiled like an idiot until he finally figured out who I was."

"And then what?" she asked as she eagerly stuffed the last of an empanada.

"We hugged like long lost friends, and he asked how I'd been. Then he did something really weird."

"What?" She stopped chewing and leaned forward with an expectant stare.

"He took hold of the top of my blouse and attempted to look down my chest. I slapped his hand off, and thank goodness the bus came 'cause I was ready to lose my femininity."

"Gawd, men can be so silly," she said, absentmindedly taking a swig of my Coke.

12

Are You Crazy?

I began to work in a hospital in upper Manhattan where I reviewed medical records for purposes of cost control, not exactly the most exciting position but one where I was responsible for no one but myself. It was there that I met the next addition to my band of bandidas.

Maddie was a curvy stack of sweetness and naiveté whose bubbly Betty Boop personality made her very popular. She knew everybody and everyone knew her. Low and dirty was the person who would knowingly hurt Maddie, for she was as soft and innocent as the day she was born.

Low and dirty was the deceptive swine named Fritz who saw her when he felt like it and had no time for her tears. So the rest of us spitfire vixens took her under our wings and proceeded to educate her in the ways of women experienced in sorting out the good, the bad, and the ugly. Or so we thought.

It's funny how much easier it is to see others' shortcomings and give advice when you're not personally involved, for it's almost impossible to see the light when you're swimming in shit.

Any suggestion of male bashing here is purely unintentional. It's not them, it's us. As I am not a scholar in psychoanalytic theory, I will not endeavor to explain why some of us are attracted to losers while rejecting righteous suitors. It just is. Eventually, some of us get it, and some of us don't.

It took me a long time to question my choices and actions, and by the time I reached that level, the best years of my life had gone by. My only regret is not having rummaged through my baggage sooner, separating the good from the useless, and learning to recognize the difference.

"Mira Maddie, regardless of what you think of yourself, you're a beautiful girl and you don't deserve to be treated like that," I said to her fuming when she revealed that Fritz had moved in with the other woman but was still making late night visits to Maddie.

"But Isabel, I still have feelings for him, and it's hard to just put them aside and forget about all the good times we've had."

"Listen, Maddie," interjected Maria, "I've been there, done that, and had the bag of platanitos. That guy is using you 'cause he knows he can. When he's finished walking all over you, he's going to split and not look back 'cause that's the way users are. When was the last time he took you out for a meal or a movie or treated you like a lady?" she asked, doing her famous neck roll, eyes bulging and lips puckered.

"Well, he did take me out for a late night meal last month, which was kinda nice. But he said he didn't want to run into her 'cause she's mean and he doesn't know how to get out of the relationship."

"Ugh!" we all screamed in unison and began to talk all at once.

"Is she threatening him?" asked Olga.

"She's got a gun to his head?" asked Janet.

"Doesn't he have any cojones?" asked Maria.

"You really believe him?" cut in Janet.

"Maddie, Fritz wants to have his cake and eat it too. And while you're wasting your life sitting by the phone and powdering your coochie in case he shows up, life and loads of decent, deserving men are passing you by. Let Fritz go and give yourself the chance to meet someone who's worthy of you. Do you not think that you deserve to be happy?"

"Oh now, preach ON, Miss Isabel!" yelled Maria, hands up in the air.

"Yes! Dee-serve to be happy!" jumped up Janet.

"Worthy, Lord, is she worthy?" witnessed Olga.

We pulled Maddie to her feet and encircled her.

"San Miguel, turn this woman around and let her see the light," preached Maria as she held her hand over Maddie's head.

"Yemayá, please slap some sense back into her since Fritz has obviously slapped it out of her. Guard her from him and keep him away. Get rid of him, Yemaya!" implored Janet, as she grabbed an invisible curse from her shoulder, threw it to the ground, and stomped on it.

"And while you're at it, send some good men our way," I added.

"Amen!" shouted the congregation as we all fell about laughing.

Saturday at the Corso nightclub, the atmosphere was electrifying and deafeningly loud as the king of the congas, Ray Baretto, banged his hard hands on the skins to the tune of "Indestructible." We sat at a table near the bar, our favorite spot for man-gazing and getting noticed. All of us got asked to dance the next number, but I decided to sit one out.

From the milling crowd of handsome men with exposed chests emerged a nice-looking guy, impeccably dressed, every hair in place, bathed in the seductive scent of Aramis. Nothing makes a man more appealing and sensual than a splash of come-hither cologne.

"Hi," said the cutie with a bewitching smile. "I noticed your friends have gone to dance and left you alone. Can I sit with you?"

"Sure," I said, not sure at all if I wanted to be tied down with someone this early in the evening. "You'll have to get up when they come back, though."

"Okay. So what's your name?" he asked loudly, trying to be heard over the noise as he sat next to me.

"Isabel. What's yours?" I yelled back.

"Eron."

I sat closer and asked him to spell it. "That's a weird name for a Puerto Rican!" I said.

"I think my mother was trying to name me Aaron but didn't know how to spell it, so I'm stuck with Eron."

Mmm-Mm, that smile sure is sexy. "So, how long have you been here?" I asked him.

"Oh, about an hour."

"No, I meant how long have you been in New York? I noticed you have an island accent, not a New York accent."

"Oh. I moved here from Puerto Rico a year ago. I was actually born in Brooklyn but my parents moved us back to Puerto Rico when I was fifteen and my brother fourteen. Anyway, I lost my job there and had a hard time finding another one, so I came back to New York to try my luck," he said.

"So are you working now?" I asked.

"Yeah, I am. I'm a security guard at a hospital in Harlem."

"No kiddin'," I said. "I work in a hospital too. Which one?"

"Hospital for Joint Diseases, over on 124th Street."

"Getouttahere! That's where I work! I've never seen you there."

"I work mostly outdoors, driving the employees' van back and forth from the hospital to the subway station. Maybe that's why. Hey, here come your friends. Wanna go over to the bar and get a drink?"

"Sure, let's go!"

We had drinks and talked until the nightclub closed. Afterwards, he said good-night and promised to look me up at the hospital.

The girls and I went to our favorite all night eatery, La Mano de Oro, for some late night munchies.

"Okay, so who is he and how was he?" Maria asked as we waited for our orders.

"Oh, just some guy who says he works where Maddie and I work."

"Really! What's his name?" pried Maddie.

"Eron, spelled E-R-O-N."

"Eron! What kinda name is that for a Puerto Rican?" asked Olga.

"Funny you should ask," I said laughing. "He was kind of boring, really."

"Boring! Girl, you wasted the whole night with a boring guy?" asked Janet. A tired looking waiter planted dishes piled with fried appetizers, and we all dug in.

"Well, he's far from being an intellectual, and we don't seem to have a lot in common. He doesn't even dance well," I said, chomping on a morsel of morcilla.

"Oh no. He can't dance?" asked Olga with great concern.

"He's kinda cute, though. We'll see what happens."

That Monday, as I sat at my desk busy with paperwork, a head popped in the door.

"Hey, clown!" It was Eron.

I suddenly remembered, to my sober dismay, that I had told him where I worked in the hospital. Big mistake. Every day that week, he followed me around and badgered me for my phone number and a date. He became annoying when he decided to nickname me "clown" and embarrassing when he'd shout it out in public to get my attention. I finally forced myself to give in. Admittedly, his relentless admiration was a first for me, and I was vaguely flattered by it.

Friday night, I let him visit with me at my apartment. We sat on the floor and shared a bottle of wine while listening to some great salsa and talking trivia. I told with him about some of the places I'd been and things I'd done, not to impress him but to discourage him from thinking that we might even remotely be compatible.

"Wow, you've had an interesting life. So what kinds of music do you like besides salsa?" he wanted to know.

"Oh, I like to listen to classical music sometimes; a little Bach, some Mozart, Thelonious Monk." I thought I'd throw the clinker in to see if he would catch it. He didn't.

"I'll bet you like to read a lot too." Maybe the rows of books on my shelves clued him in?

"I sure do! I'll read anything from books to tea leaves."

"Ah, now you're playing with me, clown," he laughed. "You're really funny, though. I like your sense of humor."

Okay, so tooting my own horn wasn't working with relentless. In an ironic twist of fate, I began to see him in a different light. His naiveté became endearing, as if his gullibility had brought out a child-like quality in him that begged to be nurtured and protected. After all, he was alone in New York—no parents, no family.

Suddenly I found myself flat on the floor, his lips pressing down on mine. "Wait a minute! Wait a minute!" I yelled, pushing him away.

"What? What?" he echoed back, with a look of astonishment.

"Shouldn't you be asking my permission to kiss me?"

"Okay, can I kiss you?"

"Oh, I guess."

He came at me like a dehydrated nomad in a desert who'd just come upon an oasis. There was nothing sweet or sensual in his advance but a ravenous lip sucking marathon with intermittent pauses to come up for air.

The wine insidiously took over, dulling the senses and numbing my dehydrated lips. As the sun went down and the room darkened, the endless kissing finally turned into an awkward fumbling with buttons and zippers and clothes being shed, lips still glued together. Marvin Gaye's "Let's Get It On" dropped onto the record player, its seductive balladry adding steaminess to an already sizzling atmosphere.

Two minutes later, it was over. Marvin Gaye's sultry voice faded as my erotic fervor wilted like a rose in desert heat.

"Oh no, not again," groaned Janet as I recounted all the sordid details of my latest fiasco.

"What's up with these impotent men you keep running into?" Maria demanded to know, as if I could tell by the length of their pinkies whether or not they had a performance issue.

"He's not impotent Maria, just overzealous, maybe."

"Are you going to see Speedy Gonzalez again?" Maddie asked with a smirk.

"Honestly, he sorta grew on me." Their thunderous laughter evinced their dirty minds. "Oh shut up! Seriously, he seems like a nice enough guy. He's not very worldly, but there's something about him that's irresistible. Maybe it's his puppy eyes or his sweet smile or maybe it's the fact that he's alone out here and needs a friend. I don't know."

"Sounds to me like he needs some sexual therapy and you need psychotherapy," suggested Maria. "Just be careful. Some of these good ol' boys have the devil in them."

"Ain't that the truth!" Maddie concurred.

Two months into our relationship, on a sweltering June day, Eron and I were sitting in the hospital van, which we often hijacked to a quiet residential street and parked under the shade of a maple tree. A faint torrid breeze stirred the leaves of the overgrown maple to rustle lazily under the scorching hot sun. Eron handed me a loaded ham and cheese sandwich and an ice cold bottle of soda.

After a long silent pause, he said, "I think we should get married."

I felt the morsel of bread get stuck in my throat. Quickly, I took a big gulp of cola to wash it down. "What did you just say?" I looked at him so I could read his lips as he repeated the words, just to make sure I had gotten it right.

"I said I think we should get married."

"Eron, why would you wanna do that? You barely know me!"

"Oh, I do know you, clown. I think we were meant to be together. This may sound corny to you, but I think we should get married so that God can bless our relationship."

It was corny, but oh, so touching. "Aww, that is so sweet," I said as I gently landed a kiss on his lips.

"I think we might as well move in together," he said. "Why don't you move into my place since the rent is cheaper? I know the apartment is smaller, but we don't really need much room, and we could save money that way."

"Okay," I said, licking the mayo from my fingers. Just like that, the pact was sealed.

The following weekend, I moved into Eron's studio apartment, and shortly after that, we began to plan our wedding. We set a date in late August of 1976, exactly four months from the day we met.

It never occurred to me to question his sincerity nor my sanity in giving in to such a weighty decision so quickly. I was ready to settle down, and it might as well be with him.

Saturday evening, following my move to Eron's place, we decided to go out to the movies and dinner. We boarded a bus up the Grand Concourse toward the Fordham RKO Theater to watch one of his favorite kung fu movies.

At one stop, in slithered a raven-haired vamp who daintily perched herself on the seat directly in front of us. Eron's eyes appeared to bulge like those comical glasses with eyeballs that spring forward and bounce off the frame. I could tolerate his looking once, but the frozen dead stare was downright disrespectful. What was worse, upon sensing my fiancé's eyeballs stuck to her cleavage, the bimbette began to coyly look back, batting her heavily mascara'd eyelashes in his direction.

"Excuse me," I interrupted him, tapping on his shoulder. "Why are you staring?"

"What are you talking about?"

"Why are you staring at that girl across from us?"

"I'm not staring at anybody!" he said, getting cross. "I'm just looking out the window."

Could I possibly been mistaken? Was he really looking out the window behind her? I decided to give him the benefit of the doubt while keeping one eye diverted in his direction. Thirty seconds later, he resumed the hypnotic look in Maybelline's direction, this time with a lecherous smirk. I looked directly at him, but even my laser beam stare didn't break his trance.

"You *are* staring, you jerk!" I whispered one decibel below a shout as I punched his shoulder. "That's so rude of you!"

"What's the matter with you? Are you crazy? I'm not staring at anybody!"

Jezebel smiled coquettishly, as if having a great time with our bickering. I gave her the evil eye.

"You do that one more time and I'm getting off this bus," I threatened.

"Relax. I'll look out another window then," he said. At that moment, the floozy sashayed off the bus, giving Eron a final flirty smile.

At the movie theater, we grabbed some munchies and sat down to watch the flick. Soon as the lights went out, Eron lit up what I thought was a cigarette, until the smell of reefer hit me like a waft of exhaust fumes.

"What the hell are you doing?" I asked.

"Smoking some weed. Want some?"

"Hell no! Put that out before somebody notices and gets us arrested!"

"Aw, come on, clown. Here, have some. Maybe it'll help you calm down."

"No, Eron. Don't be lame! Put it out...and stop calling me clown!"

"Sshhhh," somebody hushed a few rows down.

"Isabel, everybody does it. See, those guys behind us are smoking. Stop worrying!"

I watched the movie in a state of panic and was relieved when it finally ended and the lights went up.

That evening, we discussed the preparations for our wedding. Without enough time and money to plan anything elaborate, we decided to rent a cheap hall that mother had found on 149th Street in the South Bronx. At least it was close to the train station so that people could easily get there. Mother offered to supply the food while a friend recommended a DJ to provide the music.

A couple of weeks later, Maria invited us to her place for dinner. She led me into her kitchen after secretly dismissing Eron. I was shocked when a bunch of familiar faces jumped up from hiding places yelling, "Surprise!" I couldn't believe it! All of my dearest friends were there to celebrate my transition to committed woman.

For me, it marked the end of my wild, free-spirited days with a carte blanche agenda. My posse would move on without me and I without them, for I knew that by committing my life to Eron, my steadfast relationship with my friends would change dramatically. Oh, I knew they would always be there, but my loyalty would now belong to Eron first and foremost.

"Why are you crying?" asked Maria, holding my fourth forced mixed drink in her hand. I'm going to miss you girls," I sobbed.

"Aww, you know we'll always be here for you," said Janet.

"But it's not going to be the same!" I was now bawling like a toddler with a broken toy. I think the drinks had a lot to do with it.

"Here," Olga said with trembling voice. She handed me a tissue as she grabbed another and blew her nose.

"Get a grip, Isabel. This is supposed to be the happiest day of your life. What do the rest of us have to look forward to? You found your soulmate. Now have another drink and be happy," said Maria. "Here's to Isabel, may you have a long and happy life together," she toasted.

"Salud!"

Eron's parents, Don Pedro and Doña Edilia, arrived from Puerto Rico the night before the wedding. Don Pedro, a short stout gentleman with an unpretentious smile beneath a thin mustache, greeted me with a warm hug.

"It's a pleasure to meet you, Isabel" he said.

Doña Edilia gave me a cursory hug. "Ay, Dios mio, it was such a long trip! My feet are aching so, and I have such a splitting headache!" she griped in Spanish.

"Would you like some Tylenol?" I offered.

"No, I took some at the airport an hour ago, and it's still not getting rid of it."

"How about some tea?"

"No, I don't really care much for tea."

"A cup of coffee maybe? I can brew a fresh pot for you."

"No, gracias. I've had so much coffee today, I feel nauseous."

"Maybe you need some food in your stomach," I said. "Eron and I want to take you and Don Pedro out for dinner, if it's okay with you."

"Let me lie down for a while, and I'll see how I feel later."

I got her a pillow and blanket, and she lay down on the sofa while Eron, his father, and I had a pleasant chat at the kitchen table.

We had dinner later that evening at a quaint local Spanish restaurant. Eron and I ordered some beef stew over yellow rice and his father opted for stewed codfish with green plantains in keeping with his diabetic diet.

"What would you like, Mami?" he asked his mother.

"*No sé*. I don't know what to pick. Everything looks so unappetizing," she said perusing the menu.

"Mami, there's got to be something in this whole menu that you like. Want to try the same thing we're having?" Eron suggested.

"Ay, no. All that salsa will give me heartburn. As it is right now, I'm still feeling nauseous."

I decided to stay out of this one as my patience was running thin. I couldn't trust myself to speak without reaching across the table and choking her.

"How about something simple like what Papi's having?"

"No, the smell of the fish alone will make me retch. Why do they always print these menus with such small letters? I can barely read it!" Doña Edilia said, searching for her glasses.

"Mami, please make up your mind because we're all starving, and the waiter can't wait forever."

She began to slowly scrutinize the four page menu as we all waited in silence.

"Mami, a little longer and we can go straight to church for the wedding." Eron's father and I snickered.

"*Esta bien*, Eron. I will have the mofongo but without gravy and no pork rinds in it."

One week, Isabel. Just one week.

The big day finally arrived. My bridesmaids looked stunning, draped like Greek goddesses in off-white tunic dresses with flowing trousers and floral garlands in their hair. Among the ushers were my brothers Gil and Edwin, now handsome teen-agers and looking very dapper in their tuxedos. My little sister Bernie was cute as button as the flower girl.

An elegant, spit-shined black Cadillac drove Mother, little Bernie and me to St. Lucy's Church on 104th Street, the same church where Wanda and I had done our first communion and where my sister had been married. Several vehicles carrying my bridesmaids, ushers, and a few guests followed.

Ignoring traditional convention, I chose to have my mother give me away. Wearing a simple aqua gown and her hair up in curls, Mother stood next to me at the back of the church as we waited for the processional to begin. Through the haze of the sheer bridal veil, I could see old Father Galdos' smile as he waited at the altar.

Eron stood tall and handsome next to his best man Joe, his face radiant, his brilliant smile emitting rays of incandescent joy.

As they had done so many times before in other places and circumstances, my best friends walked before me and led the way to my rightful place, leaving no doubt that this is where I now belonged, with Eron.

At the altar, Mother lifted my veil and gently kissed my forehead. I looked into her teary eyes and said, "Thank you for everything, Mother."

With a tremulous voice, she said, "*Que Dios te bendiga, mi hija.*" May God bless you, my daughter. She quickly turned away and took her seat.

I turned towards Eron and realized why he seemed to glow from the back of the church. His eyes were as glassy as marbles with a tinge of sanguine red. His pale lips were quivering, his face flushed to a shine.

Father Galdos began the ceremony in his beautiful Castilian accent, but his words faded as bittersweet recollections and doubts invaded my thoughts. *God I'm going to miss my friends! What the hell am I doing? Do I really love this man?* Too late for all of that now. I started to cry.

Father Galdos stopped the sermon midway. "Are you okay, Isabel?"

"Yes, I'm okay," I said. Eron looked at me puzzled. I managed to keep a smile glued on through the rest of the ceremony.

After the tiresome posing for pictures at the photographer's studio, we headed back to the South Bronx for the reception. Eron and I waited outside the hall's entrance for his parents while my family and friends went inside.

This was a low-budget, quickie wedding, not exactly what every girl dreams of. There were no glitzy lights or cameras waiting anxiously for our arrival; no banquet tables loaded with canapés or hors d'oeuvres, no towering wedding cake. No one announced our arrival to thunderous applause and raised champagne glasses.

I had gone to the reception hall the morning of the wedding. Saddled with bags full of tablecloths and candles, I walked up a steep narrow staircase into a dark cavernous room with several wooden tables and chairs. Tall windows were covered with dusty red velvet curtains which overlooked the elevated third avenue subway and crowded street below. I moved the heavy curtains aside to let in some light, and a cloud of grit fell on me like fairy dust with a scent of soot. It was too late to feel disappointment or regrets.

I quickly got to work covering and decorating the stained tables. A long table would serve as the seating area for the bridal party and another table was decorated for the food and cake that Mother had volunteered to provide. Sweaty and soot-stained, I looked around and was pleased with what I had accomplished.

When Eron, his parents, and I arrived at the hall that evening, there were a few guests already seated. I looked over at the buffet area and saw a large bone on a plate with a few morsels of unknown meat stuck to it, a large bowl with lettuce and tomatoes, and a large tin pan half-filled with yellow rice and pigeon peas. I almost missed the two-tiered wedding cake my mother had bought from Valencia Bakery sitting solitary on the bridal table. My heart sank. I prayed no one else would show up.

Thank goodness the DJ was already there, cranking up what sounded like lively foot-stomping music. No one was dancing.

"Get me a drink," I said to Eron while looking around in dismay.

Eron returned and handed me a rum and coke. "I'm going to make a quick run with Joe. I'll be right back," he said.

"Where are you going?"

"I'm just going with him to pick up his friend," he said.

"Great," I said sarcastically. "Just don't take too long."

I sat at a table, fairly sloshed after downing a few stiff drinks and happy to feel no pain. It was comforting to see my friends having a good time dancing with each other as there were no unattached males available.

Peering at my watch, I realized that Eron had now been gone for 2 ½ hours. As I slurred good bye to some of my guests, in sauntered the shameless groom, unabashedly high.

"Where the hell have you been?" I asked.

"I'm really sorry. Joe's friend wasn't ready, so we had a few drinks while we waited. Please don't be angry, Isabel. I didn't have a choice."

"Jesus, Eron, it's our wedding day! Couldn't Joe tell his friend to take a cab? This is so embarrassing! Everyone's been asking for you!"

"Isabel, like you said, it's our wedding day. Lighten up! C'mon, let's dance."

On our first wedding night, we passed out on a cold bathroom floor while his parents slept on the sofa bed.

Eron's parents returned the following week to Puerto Rico, and we settled down to enjoy conjugal bliss.

"Eron, what are you staring at?"

"What the hell are you talking about? I'm not staring at anyone!"

"Yes, you are! I'm looking right at you, fool! Don't you understand how disrespectful that is to me?"

"Don't you understand how annoying you are to me? I'm not looking at anybody! What is your problem, Isabel?"

"My problem is you! And stop smoking that damn reefer! You're becoming a pothead, and it's killing your brain cells."

It got to the point where I dreaded going out with him, and when we did, I often chose to ignore his habits. I was knocking my head against the wall, and all I was getting for it was a terrible headache.

Eron got fired from his security job at the hospital for insubordination and soon after became employed in the garment district, assembling costume jewelry. He was able to bring work home, and oftentimes after dinner, we would sit together at the kitchen table and interlock the links with pliers until our hands hurt.

It was at these times that Eron and I were able to have pleasant conversations and share our thoughts civilly.

"Eron, you're a smart guy and you deserve to be doing better than this. Have you ever thought about going to college?" I asked one day.

"Yeah, I would consider that, but how are we going to manage financially?"

"Well, right now I make enough money so that you could work part-time and go to school part-time, then see how it goes. How does that sound?"

"I could give it a try, I guess. I'm not really sure what I would study, though."

For the next few weeks, I sent for college catalogs, and together we went over several career options. He finally decided that working with numbers and finances would be of interest to him, and he settled on accounting.

That fall, Eron started attending Manhattan Community College in the evenings while still employed at the costume jewelry sweatshop. I was impressed with the way he submerged himself into his studies with conviction and drive.

He was the only man I knew who could focus and complete his assignments on time in spite of the weed that was melting his brain. I conjectured that maybe focusing on smart projects could possibly slow down the process of brain cell destruction. It's the only way I can explain the phenomenon.

I left my job at the hospital for a more challenging position, much to Maddie's dismay and my great sadness. Over the past two years, I had lost touch with my posse, and now Maddie was about to become a memory too.

Through my old connections at the hospital, I was able to get Eron a paid internship in the accounting department where he worked full-time while attending school in the evenings. No more assembling cheap jewelry late into the night.

I became superwoman, cooking three-course meals for Eron, keeping the apartment spotless; washing, ironing, shopping; work, bills. I saw how dedicated he was to his responsibilities, and I felt that I needed to do my part as well. But although I often told him how proud I was of him, the sentiment was never reciprocated.

"Eron, how was dinner? Did you like it?"

"It was nice."

"Eron, how do I look? Do you like this dress? It's new."

"It looks all right."

"Eron, how come you never compliment me or show any appreciation for what I do?"

He looked up from his books, a stern look on his face. "What are you talking about? I appreciate what you do."

"But you never say anything. How would I know that?"

"Why do I need to say anything for something that you're supposed to do? You're a married woman now, in case you haven't noticed."

Oh no, he didn't.

"I'm also a human being who would like to feel appreciated once in a while," I said near tears. "And if you gave me half the attention you give to strange women on the street, maybe I wouldn't feel so worthless."

Banging on the table, "Isabel, my mother raised two children while my father worked, and she never complained!"

"She sure complains a lot about it now! She told me she was never happy with your father!"

Eron stood up and came at me, hands clenched at his sides. "Don't you ever talk about my parents like that again, you hear me?"

I knew when it was time to stop, and that was it. Once again, I found myself figuratively pasting stars on a stark bathroom wall.

In 1978, I began working as a medical terminology teacher for a wonderful program in El Barrio that trained unskilled people as medical transcribers. Oddly, it was located in the very same building where the Soul & Latin Theater of my youth once had its headquarters.

This would be yet another mystifying example of fated events. It would turn out to be the most gratifying job I'd ever had and one that would more than make up for the lackluster life I led at home.

Through the warped threshold of that dilapidated building entered the underprivileged and destitute, looking for a skill and the chance for a better life. We put them through a rigorous screening process and a demanding two-week orientation.

How some managed to balance their busy home lives and personal challenges with the rigors of the program was beyond me. But in the end, those who toughed it out left with an invaluable skill and a heightened sense of accomplishment and self-worth. At graduation time, I don't know who was prouder, them or us.

Eventually I became Assistant Coordinator of the program and, as such, was privy to many of the students' personal misfortunes and dilemmas.

Rosa was a quiet, reserved twenty-seven-year-old single mother of three boys. Like everyone else, she struggled through the program, but her poor English language skills provided an even greater challenge for her.

"Rosa, how do you do it? How do you manage to stay focused on your studies and take care of your three boys at the same time?" I asked her.

"Well, I do it for them, for my boys," she answered in her thick Spanish accent. "I want them to have a better life and to make a good example. Maybe someday we can move from the projects to a nice home where they can have one room each and good friends to play." Her sad hazel eyes clouded with tears as she spoke of them.

"Tell me about your boys, Rosa."

She cleared her throat and collected herself before answering. "Well, Manuel, he is six and he love to color and paint. Jose is four and he is very lively and talkative. My oldest son, Roberto, he is ten, and he is very quiet and stays alone a lot."

"Where is their father?" I asked.

"Jose and Manuel's father left one year ago. He always picking on the oldest, Roberto, and we have many fights. You see, Roberto has a different father. Roberto's father was dark skin and had frizzy hair, just like my boy. He look very different than his brothers. Sometimes his brothers and cousins pick on him too because he look different.

"Roberto's father was on drugs and he beat me many times and stole from me. He die from the drugs." The tears began to flow, cascading like rivulets down her flawless face.

"I love all my boys, but I have a special place in my heart for Robertito."

"Rosa, I really admire your courage and the strength you have shown in wanting to better your life for you and your boys. You haven't given up, even though I know this is hard for you. I want you to know that I am very proud of you and that we are here to help you in any way we can so that you can finish the program and get a good job. You and your children deserve a better life. This is your chance."

"Thank you, Isabel. I really appreciate that."

Luz, who preferred to be called Lucky, was on the opposite end of the spectrum—way opposite and off the chart. An outspoken Latina whose indelicate vernacular could put a drunken sailor to shame, no one dared confront this untamed shrew for, in a war of words, they would never win.

In her mid-thirties and the single mother of two young girls, Lucky was the epitome of voluptuous womanhood, yet she often described herself as "fat and ugly." Heaven forbid one should argue that point with her. She was definitely a challenge.

"Lucky, I noticed that you didn't complete your last two home assignments. Can you tell me..."

"Listen, I've been having a lot of problems at home lately. My oldest daughter isn't doing well in school, so I went to see her teacher and come to find out the bitch hasn't been going to school. I kicked her ass soon as she got home. But now I gotta watch her. She keeps that shit up, I'm sending her back to her father.

"And that son-of-a bitch boyfriend of mine won't leave his wife, and I'm up to here with his bullshit lies. Last week he came to dinner and gave me another sorry-assed story about his wife being sick, and he couldn't stay over. That's when I picked up the frying pan and threw it at him, fried chicken and all, and told him to get the hell out."

"Lucky, is there anything I can do to help?" I asked, slightly overwhelmed.

"Yeah. Got any friends who can whack that lying bastard for me?"

The students in the medical transcription program started to complain about the lack of study space or a lounge where they could have lunch and review their notes. It was a fair request, but as a government-sponsored program, we didn't have the financial means to furnish a space for that purpose.

At the next staff meeting, I came up with one of my demented ideas for a fundraiser, hoping to get everyone on my wacky bandwagon.

"Guys, as some of you may know, the students have been asking for a lounge, and I've come up with an idea to raise money for furnishings."

Seven pairs of eyes stared at me in total silence.

"Let's put on a show featuring groups of the sixties. We could use the community center as a venue, which holds about 200 people. With good advertising, we could make enough money to furnish the lounge and then some. What do you think?"

George, my administrative assistant, looked at me incredulously. "Isabel, from where would we get the performers?"

"Well, George, you're looking at them," I said.

"What!" echoed down the line in a domino effect.

"Folks, here's your chance to be your favorite singer in front of a live audience for a good cause. You can do a solo act or be part of a group. Since it's for their benefit, let's involve the students. Heck, we could ask the other program staff members in the building and see if anyone would be interested in joining us."

"Oh, my goodness. It's a crazy idea but doable," said one of my teachers.

"I can do Mary Wells!"

"We could be the Temptations!"

"We should have outfits like they wore in the sixties."

"But I can't sing!"

"Well," I said, "if you don't feel comfortable singing, there are plenty of other things you could do like help with advertisements, organizing, or selling tickets."

"What would we do for a sound system?"

"I could ask Johnny Colon at the music school across the street," suggested George. "Maybe he'd be willing to lend us his equipment."

"Okay, George, you can be in charge of that. Since it sounds like everyone's on board, please come up with some ideas for acts, and let's discuss them on Monday," I said over the commotion.

For the next few weeks, the event sparked a flurry of activity and excitement. After school, students and staff could be heard practicing their songs and dance steps. Some of the participants created costumes for their groups. Meanwhile, the publicity committee created a buzz in the community, and tickets started selling like hotcakes.

On the day of the event, ticket holders were lined up early, and by the time the show started, it was standing room only.

Johnny Colon, the great Latin musician and music teacher, graciously loaned us his equipment and ran the sound system for us.

"Ladies and gentlemen, put your hands together for...The Supremes!" Three beautiful girls dressed identically in blue satin dresses made their entrance to tumultuous applause.

For one magical night, people lived out their fantasies, and the audience, having become enmeshed in the illusion, lavished the performers with resounding accolades.

To a great extent, it was my fantasy, to relive the moments that brought me joy through music. It was a chance to stand in shoes I'd never wear, to adulate figments of idols I'd never see.

"And now, get ready for the Queen of Latin Soul, La Yiyiyi herself," said the announcer.

For my performance, I chose to emulate La Lupe, a Cuban-born singer who enraptured audiences with her raspy, soulful ballads and fiery salsa songs. Her unique interpretation of songs manifested itself in sensual, energetic, sometimes manic performances that stunned and captivated her followers. She'd tear at her hair, beat her chest, collapse on the floor, and throw articles of nonessential clothing and jewelry to the audience. It was as if the music possessed her, and her body unreservedly interpreted the emotions behind the lyrics. Her voice stood out as one of the most passionate and electrifying vocals I had ever heard.

"Ladies and gentlemen...La Lupe!"

The initial sounds of her guttural laughter on the song "Fever" were drowned by the audience's rowdy ovation. The second I stepped onstage, I became La Lupe. Driven by the crowd's cheers, I belted out her song, and when it reached its crescendo and the backup singers hit the chorus, off came my shawl, earrings and heels, which I threw into the audience, to their great delight.

The ovation was overwhelming, the moment unforgettable.

Our show was a huge success, and we made enough money to furnish a student lounge and purchase additional typewriters for the transcribers.

The demand for a second show was so great, we decided to do another performance the following year with different acts. That event turned out to be another success, and with the profits, we purchased brand new Dictaphones for all our students.

Unfortunately, by the third year, our program experienced radical changes due to the government's takeover of all the programs, and we were never the same.

Eron and I had just finished eating dinner. It was the perfect time for me to tell him the news.

"Eron..." I paused to make sure I had his full attention.

"Yeah?"

"We're going to have a baby."

"No way! Are you sure?" His face broke out in a wide grin.

"I'm sure. I went to the doctor, and I got the call today that my pregnancy test was positive."

"Oh, Isabel." He got up in a flash and hugged me. "That's wonderful! That is just fantastic!"

For the rest of the evening, we talked and made plans for the child that would make our circle complete.

Nothing could have prepared me for the joys of pregnancy. In spite of the morning sickness and everything tasting like cardboard, I felt deliriously happy, and I made life changes to ensure that my baby would have a healthy start. A baby...I tried to picture what it might look like, smell like, sound like, but mostly what it would feel like to hold him or her.

Three months later, the nausea was diminishing, and I was finally able to taste food again. I awoke early one morning, and while Eron slept, I sat at the kitchen table with a cup of decaf, enjoying the quiet solitude and daydreaming about the months to come. The coffee quickly worked its way to my bladder, and I went to relieve myself. When I got up to flush, the toilet water was beet red.

"Eron! Eron!" I screamed.

After Eron calmed me down, he paged Dr. Haynes, my obstetrician, who answered our call almost immediately. I explained to him what was happening.

"Isabel, this may be some breakthrough bleeding, but I want you to lie down for the rest of the day. Stay as calm and quiet as possible and come see me first thing tomorrow morning."

The next morning, I had an ultrasound, and as I waited to get the results, I silently prayed for another miracle.

I sat in front of my doctor and searched his kind face for some semblance of hope. In his soothing, West Indian voice, he said, "Isabel, it looks like an impending abortion. The pregnancy has begun to detach itself and will eventually be expelled."

The feeling of loss was overwhelming. The shattered dream of a life created was now disintegrating and being disposed of like human waste. What did I do wrong? Why?

Dr. Haynes must have read my thoughts. "There is nothing you could have done to prevent something like this. Sometimes the embryo doesn't develop properly, and this is nature's way of ending a pregnancy that is not viable. Go home, rest, stay calm. Keep yourself well hydrated. If there are any changes, give me a call."

The pain began as soon as I left my doctor's office. Instead of going home, I went to Mother's place for I didn't want to be alone. Mother made me a nice cup of ginger tea while Grandma, using her healing hands, gently massaged my belly, softly praying. But the cramps intensified, and I knew that my body was now forcefully expelling what was left of my illusion.

Within an hour, it was all over.

Eron picked me up at Mother's house late that evening and took me home in a cab.

"I'm so sorry, Isabel. I know you really wanted this baby."

"Didn't you?" I asked, wanting to elicit some emotion from him, a soothing thought, some sympathy.

"Yeah, but maybe it was meant to happen. Maybe this wasn't the right time. We can always try again."

I supposed he had a point, but I was too distraught to dwell on it. First, I needed time to heal.

"Hi... Isabel?"

I immediately recognized my supervisor's voice at the other end of the phone line and wondered why he was calling me on a Saturday morning.

"Hi Bruce, what's up?"

"Isabel, I'm afraid I have some bad news for you."

"Oh Lord, what's happened?"

"I don't know how else to say this. One of little Rosa's boys has died."

"What? Rosa's boy? What happened?"

"There's been a tragic accident. Apparently when she got home from school, she caught the boy hanging out the window, spitting. She yelled out to him, and the shock of her voice must have made his hands slip on the sill, and he fell out, thirteen floors."

"Oh no...no, no, no!" That poor girl, after all she'd been through and now this. I needed to know. "Bruce, which one?"

"The eldest, Roberto."

What a cruel twist of fate! I couldn't begin to imagine how Rosa would cope with this tragedy. The loss of a child—is there a greater sorrow than the loss of part of oneself?

"His viewing is tonight at Ortiz's Funeral Home on 103rd Street."

"I'll be there," I said.

All along the train ride to El Barrio, a place where dreams lived and died amidst the shambles of its decaying tenements, I thought of Rosa and prayed that her dreams would not die with Roberto.

Inside the somber funeral home, groups of people gathered in corners in hushed conversation, as if speaking in a decibel above a whisper would awaken the sleeping child. I furtively looked inside the parlor searching for Rosa and quickly turned away as I beheld the small coffin where her child lay at rest. I could not bear to look at him.

"Have you seen Rosa?" I asked a group of mourners.

"No, she's not here yet."

I sat on a bench facing the entrance, grateful for a few moments to gather my thoughts. What could I possibly say to her to lessen her pain? What befitting words could I use to convey my deep sadness for her irredeemable loss?

I thought of the words of condolence people often use in their own awkwardness—empty verbiage uttered by rote and familiarity: "He's in a better place now; she's not suffering anymore; you must be strong for your family; you can have another one; call me if you need anything; *te acompaño en tus sentimientos* (I am with you in your sorrow)."

I decided to say what I felt when the moment came. No fancy sayings, no worn-out phrases, no sappy conjectures.

Rosa walked in through the main doors and slowly made her way up the steps, eyes sunken, her porcelain skin now pallid, her visage trance-like. Our eyes met, and as she drew closer, her face contorted into a mask of pain and grief. We held onto each other and cried, her pain osmosing right through me.

"I am so, so sorry, Rosa. My heart is breaking for you. I am so very sorry."

I led her back to the bench, and we held hands as I listened to her recount the sordid details of little Roberto's death, as if recalling made it that much more real for her.

"I don't know how I can continue with school. It will be too hard for me, I think," she said.

"Rosa, please don't give up. It will be hard, but you are so close to finishing. Remember the dreams you had, and even though Roberto is not here, you still have two beautiful boys who are counting on you to make that wish come true for them. Do it for yourself, for Roberto, and for your boys. I promise you, we will help you in every way possible to make it happen. I know this is too much to think about right now. I would like to come see you in a few days, if it's okay with you."

"Yes, that would be very nice. Thank you so much for coming," she said as she stood and gave me a final hug.

A few months later, with her two little boys sitting in the audience in their Sunday best, Rosa proudly received her certificate as an accomplished medical transcriber and, soon after, was hired by a group of physicians in Manhattan. Eventually, she was able to move out of the projects into a better neighborhood.

I lost touch with Rosa after a few years, but I have no doubt that wherever she is, she is living out her dreams.

The sudden jab in my belly awoke me from a deep slumber. I turned over and looked at the clock. It was 5:00 a.m.

I placed my hand over my round belly and waited to feel its changing contour as the baby stretched an arm or a leg. A few minutes later, another jab, but this time, my abdomen became firm as it painfully contracted.

I rolled out of bed and made myself a cup of chamomile tea. No sense in waking Eron so early for a false alarm. He'd be up in an hour anyway to get ready for work.

Another painful contraction took my breath away. They were now coming ten minutes apart like clockwork.

"Eron...Eron," I gently called as I gripped the back of a chair.

"Huh?" he answered groggily, without moving.

"Eron, I think it's time."

"Time for what?" he asked, still not moving.

"Time to have the baby."

"What!" he yelled, sitting bolt upright, covers tossed aside. "Are you sure?"

"I think so," I said as another bolt hit me.

We dressed in record time. Eron grabbed my suitcase and escorted me to the elevator. I realized, as we attempted to cross the street to our car, that the contractions had stopped.

"Wait a minute, Eron. Nothing's happening now. Maybe it was false labor. Let's go back upstairs."

"Are you sure?"

"Yeah, let's go back," I said.

We took the elevator back up, and as we approached our apartment, another excruciating contraction knocked the wind out of me.

"Wait, wait!" I yelled.

"What?"

"We'd better go."

"Are you sure?"

"Yes, I'm sure."

Back down the elevator we went, but there was no turning back now.

We got to Union Hospital, where I was rushed to the Obstetrics Unit and quickly settled in a small private room. A surly nurse brusquely examined me and informed us that I was only two centimeters dilated. I found that hard to believe as my contractions were coming five minutes apart, and the pain was intolerable.

Eron and I had attended birthing classes, where I absorbed every bit of information while he slept through most of them. There he was sitting ten feet away from me, clueless.

"Eron, for crissakes, don't just sit there! Come here and help me breathe through the contractions like we were taught!"

"Like what? What do you want me to do?"

"Just take deep breaths with me when the pain starts, like right now!" I took slow deep breaths and Eron began to do the same, but as the pain reached its climax, Eron started to hyperventilate.

"No, Eron! Breathe slower, like this!" This was just unbelievable! "Eron, just go sit back down!" He sat down again and quietly stared at me through the next violent spasm, his face the color of guacamole.

The agonizing pain, the frustration of not making progress, Eron's clumsiness—it all finally got to me. "Eron, why couldn't you have paid attention at the classes? Get out! Just get the hell out!"

"Are you sure?"

"Get out!" The next one hit me as he walked out the door.

Three weeks earlier, I had been struggling up the hill towards the Grand Concourse with a full shopping cart, when a young man approached me.

"Miss, can I help you with that?" he asked.

"No, it's okay," I answered out of breath.

"Let me help you. I can see you're having a hard time with that cart."

"Well, all right," I said as I handed the cart to him. At that point, I really didn't care if he ran off with it.

"Wow, this is really heavy. Don't you have anyone at home to help you?"

"Well yes, but he's still asleep, and I didn't want to bother him."

Yes, I had a man at home, but he would've gotten annoyed if I interrupted his beauty sleep, so I'd rather do it myself than get into an argument.

There I was, in a hospital bed, struggling alone again.

Eight hours later, the contractions were coming like unrelenting bolts of lightning, but still no progress. My obstetrician came in and informed me that I was only three centimeters dilated, and it would be in the baby's best interest to deliver it by Caesarean section. I readily agreed as by then I was completely exhausted, and the thought of being put out of my misery was a welcome relief.

"I'll go tell Eron," Dr. Sabal said. She returned a few minutes later. "Isabel, I couldn't find your husband. I tried calling your home number, but there was no answer. Do you know where I can reach him?"

"No, Dr. Sabal, I have no idea," I answered, embarrassed that my husband was nowhere to be found at a time like this.

I was wheeled into a cold operating room. A screen was placed upright and midway down my chest so that

I couldn't see what was happening below. My arms were strapped straight out from my body in a crucifixion-like pose. A masked face behind me instructed me to count backwards from one hundred. I think I got to ninety-seven before everything went black.

At some point, I began to feel my body being manipulated, and I could hear the voices in the room. I tried to vocalize that I could hear them, but no words came out.

"Ok, here it comes. It's a girl!" Dr. Sabal said. *It's a girl.* I heard a shrill cry, and the room went dark again.

I spent a few hours in recovery where a kindly nurse with a deep Irish brogue bathed me. Just as I was being wheeled out of recovery, Eron showed up, out of breath and drenched in sweat.

"Where have you been? Do you even know what we had?" I asked him.

"No. What did we have?"

"A girl. We had a girl. And where were you?"

"I went to hang out with my brother at the handball court." He had that stupid reefer-high look on his face. I was livid.

"I've been through hell here by myself, and you've been hanging out with your brother and getting high? Do you know I ended up having a Caesarean, and my doctor tried to reach you and you were nowhere to be found?"

"You had a Caesarean? Jesus, I'm really sorry, Isabel. I just didn't know what to do."

The thought that I had given birth to a child was imperceptible. I had often created mental images of what our baby might look like: his nose, my eyes; his lips, my hair, fitting pieces of our features together and mentally creating composite sketches of our baby. No amount of fantasizing could have prepared me for this moment.

The bonding was instantaneous, the love for her overwhelming. She was perfect in every way. Wrapped like a papoose, her rose red lips opened as if to cry, but no sound came. I looked at Eron, and his eyes were glistening. We held her for a few minutes before the nurse took her away.

"I'm really sorry," the nurse whispered, "but we're not supposed to bring out the babies this late. We'll bring her out to you again in the morning."

I decided to call her Aimée, French for beloved.

I wished those birthing classes had warned me about the drudgery of postpartum blues. Eron came to visit me at the hospital the next day and found me holding the baby and sobbing.

"Hey, what's the matter?" he asked.

"She won't breastfeed!" I was beside myself.

"Well, are you doing it right?"

"Of course I'm doing it right! I even had the breastfeeding expert here to make sure, but she just won't go for it!" I cried.

"It's no big deal, Isabel. Just give her a bottle."

"No big deal? Maybe not for you, but for me it is!"

For the next four weeks, I cried about my weight, my sore incision, my burned dinners, and Aimée cried right along with me. Her colic-induced wailing caused many sleepless nights.

"And this too shall pass" became my redeeming mantra and, eventually, it did.

I was lugging a cart full of laundry up the hill on my way home, when I spotted a familiar face walking towards me.

"Louie! Oh my goodness, Louie! It's so good to see you," I shrieked as I bear-hugged my cousin and childhood playmate. It had been a good ten years since I'd last seen him.

"It's good to see you too," he said, half-smiling.

Louie had changed. There was a trace of sadness in his olive eyes that once sparkled with a touch of mischief. He was unkempt, with a five o'clock shadow and scruffy clothes that hung limply on his thin frame. It was alarming to see him this way.

"How have you been?" I asked, feigning enthusiasm to conceal my concern.

"Oh, I've been all right. Just working and trying to keep myself out of trouble," he answered with a feeble chuckle.

"How's your baby?" I asked. "He must be grown by now."

"Well, his mother moved to Connecticut a few years ago, and I haven't heard from them since."

He appeared almost embarrassed to answer my probing questions, as if these were matters he'd rather not discuss. I decided to leave well enough alone. We chatted briefly about friends we hadn't seen and even shared a laugh when we reminisced about the old days.

I wanted to stay in touch with him but he told me that he didn't have a phone. I gave him my phone number and asked him to call me when he could get to one.

"I'd love to have you over for dinner and you can meet Eron and my Aimée. Promise me you'll call me," I insisted.

"Yeah, sure. I'll call you."

He never did.

Eron and I moved from the small studio into a one-bedroom apartment with a tiny kitchen but a sizable living room and bedroom. I was glad that I no longer had to pull out the sofa bed every night but was dismayed to discover that a battalion of roaches had taken over the kitchen to feast on micro morsels of pot luck edibles left behind. Some things you just can't get away from.

Never mind gas masks and fallout shelters in the event of biological warfare. Many New Yorkers move from place to place equipped with the essentials of vermin assault weaponry: mouse traps, roach spray, and sticky tapes. In some neighborhoods, it's a must.

Eron began to have a hissy fit over our dwindling finances and my lack of input, as if having a baby was akin to a seaside vacation. So I reluctantly handed over my six-week old newborn to Doña Susana, a wonderful Dominican woman who lived on the ground floor of the building, and I returned to work.

He completed his associate's degree and went on to pursue his bachelor's degree, immersing himself in his studies and often working late into the night. He pushed himself almost obsessively, wanting always to be on top of the game.

His personality gradually changed, from naïve, loud, and fun-loving to tightfisted, opinionated, and controlling. There were times when, while in conversation with a group of friends, I'd cringe with embarrassment at some of his divisive views.

When Aimée was a year old, we took her to Puerto Rico to be baptized. Eron's cousin Myrna had also given birth to a baby girl on Aimee's birthday, so we decided to baptize each other's babies on the same day.

Eron's parents lived in a small concrete house on the mountains of Utuado. Sadly, Eron's father had passed away two years before.

Like my mother, Eron's mother was never into writing and staying in touch. She visited us once when Aimée was first born and brought along her new husband. Their relationship didn't last very long as he turned out to be an alcoholic and a womanizer. When I last saw her, still in the throes of wedded bliss, she was a changed woman. I dreaded to see what she had become now that her disastrous marriage had ended.

The minute we picked up our rental car, Eron dug into his suitcase, plopped himself into the driver's seat, and lit up a joint.

"What the hell are you doing?" I asked in disbelief.

"What does it look like I'm doing? Relax, will you?"

"Eron, you mean to tell me you stashed pot in your suitcase? Are you insane? What if we got caught?"

"Well, we didn't, so settle down."

The ride up the steep mountainside to Doña Edilia's house was treacherous and nerve-wracking, with Eron sucking on his smelly sinsemilla stogie. With the windows wide open for Aimée's sake, I tried to focus instead on the beautiful views along the sides of the road.

We arrived at Doña Edilia's house just before sundown and were greeted with sober hugs and kisses. Edilia was never into overt displays of joy, no matter the circumstance. After settling in, we sat with her, and over a cup of café, listened impassively to a litany of physical ailments and the usual fatalistic commentary.

A few days later, Aimée and little Brenda were baptized in a lovely ceremony, followed by a reception in Cousin Myrna's house.

A beautiful doe-eyed girl with long brown hair naturally became the object of Eron's roving eye syndrome. I was fuming inside for his obsessive compulsion was so blatant, it was evident to everyone. I could see people looking at him then at me, as if wondering how I would react.

I had decided a while back to ignore it in case he was doing it to get a reaction from me. That obviously wasn't working.

I would often look at myself in the mirror wondering what was so wrong with me. The woman looking back was never pretty enough; eyes too small, neck too short, too fat, smile too toothy, clothes not feminine enough. Though I had never been into gobs of makeup and jewelry and sexy dresses, I began to make changes in my appearance, adapting hair, makeup and dress styles I had seen in the women he admired. That didn't work either.

Our vacation in Puerto Rico was over much too soon. On a beautiful sun-drenched morning, we began to make our way back down the mountains. Forty minutes into our car ride, Eron slammed on the brakes with an "Oh shit!"

"What? What's wrong?" I asked.

"I left my bag of weed back at Mom's house. I have to go get it," he said, turning the car around.

"Are you serious? Can't you leave it? Do you know what will happen if we get caught with drugs at the airport?"

"It'll be worst if my mother finds it," he said.

Back up the mountains we went to retrieve Eron's stash. Luckily, our vacation wasn't to include some indecorous R&R in the slammer.

Eron's addiction often led us to the seediest places, where I was forced to sit alone in the car, metaphorically fingering rosary beads and mentally reciting Hail Marys while he went out to cop some weed. Our usual Saturday errands took us to the supermarket, the butcher, the laundromat, and the drug dealer on Morris. It was unnerving.

13

Secrets

Back at Mother's house, my sister Wanda and Sammy returned to the South Bronx as Sammy was unable to find long-term employment in Naranjito. She promptly became pregnant with her first child and had three baby girls in succession. Sammy invested in a hole-in-the-wall storefront and converted it to a jukebox dive, much like the ones seen along the mountain roads on the island. I was thrilled to have my sister back.

It was then that I discovered quite by accident, that my nineteen-year-old brother Edwin, who was still in high school, had kept a few secrets from me.

Edwin had grown into a handsome young man. Of medium height and build, his skin had the creamy texture of tapioca pudding. Baby-fine brown hair and expressive big brown eyes conferred upon him an aura of gullibility and child-like playfulness.

A sweet, malleable Gumby with a heart of gold, he had a wacky gift for saying the funniest things with perfect comedic timing. In a different world, he would have been a brilliant stand-up comic. But in his world, where survival of the fittest favored those with ingrained street smarts and hardhearted toughness, my brother was a prime target for extinction.

"Edwin, what do you mean someone stole your motorcycle?" I asked him while sipping coffee at Mother's house one day. "I didn't even know you had one."

"Get this. It had no license plates. He doesn't even have a driver's license!" ratted Gilbert.

"Wait a minute. How did you get a motorcycle with no license?"

"Well, I saved a little bit of money and bought it from a friend of mine," he said.

"How did it get stolen, Edwin?"

"Some guys came up to me, showed me a knife, and told me to hand it over, so I did."

"What? Why didn't you get plates and a license for it? You do realize you can't report it and get it back, don't you?" I said, starting to get impatient with him.

"Go on Ed, tell her the truth," goaded Gilbert.

"I didn't get a license because...well...I can't read."

I almost fell out of my chair. "Edwin, you can't read at all?"

"I can read a little bit," he said, visibly embarrassed.

Realizing that I was badgering my brother and making him uncomfortable, I adopted a softer tone. "Edwin, didn't anyone at school notice that you couldn't read? How did you get this far without anyone knowing?"

"Some of them knew that I couldn't read well. They just put me in a special reading class, but it never sunk in. I just sat there and got bored with it, so I quit," he said.

"Wait a minute. What do you mean you quit?" His confession hit me like a bolt from nowhere.

"I quit school."

"He dropped out," added Gilbert, like I needed translation.

Surely someone must have seen him struggle. Someone must have noticed that his school work was not up to standards. Someone must have seen him lose focus and interest.

I was angry. Not at Edwin so much as all the people who had let him down; the school system that ignored the signs and passed him on to another grade; the family, including myself, for not asking questions; the individuals who labeled him as odd all his life and contributed to his lack of self-worth.

"Ed, read this headline for me," I instructed, as I handed him a copy of the *Daily News*. He was able to read the small words but had difficulty making out the lengthier ones, as if they were written in hieroglyphics.

I wondered if my brother was dyslexic or had some form of attention deficit disorder. I had no idea where to go from there. My little brother was lost, and I didn't know how to help him.

Edwin got involved with a fifteen-year-old girl who became obsessed with him. A year and a half later, she bore him a baby girl. He resorted to supporting his young family the only way he knew how, by selling drugs on street corners. Their youthful romance soon fizzled, as so many young relationships do.

My brother never went back to school, and the low level jobs I encouraged him to pursue didn't pay him enough to support his baby. He returned to the streets. I prayed every night for him, that the hood wouldn't swallow him up and spit out his bullet-riddled body like it had done with so many of his friends.

In a twisted turn of fate, Gilbert had been accepted into the New York City Police Academy and was about to finish his training. It was all the more reason for him not to understand, let alone forgive, his brother's descent into a life of crime.

"Hola Mami, how are things going?" I asked Mother in one of my infrequent phone calls. I only called my mother now when I had the patience to listen to her bellyache or the guts to hear bad news.

"Your Grandma is having trouble with her urine and controlling her bowels. I have my usual aches and pains but can't complain, and your brother Edwin got in trouble with the law and spent three nights in jail."

"He what? What happened?"

"I'm not even sure what happened. Here, talk to your brother," she said, handing the phone to Gilbert.

"Well sis, it's like this. Seems your knucklehead brother got caught with drugs and was carted off to jail. They gave him a break and put him on probation since he's never been in trouble before. He got off easy this time, but the next time, he'll do time in the slammer for sure."

A few months later, I got another phone call from Gilbert.

"Isabel, guess where your brother Edwin is," he asked me.

"Is he alive and okay?" I held my breath.

"Yeah," said Gilbert, "but he won't be when I get my hands on him. Get this. Edwin went to see his probation officer, and when they searched him, he had drugs on him. Edwin went to see his probation officer with drugs on him! I can't believe he could be that stupid!"

"Oh my God! What's going to happen to him now, Gil? Where is he?"

"Where the hell do you think he is? They cuffed him and sent him to prison. He's going to do at least a year if not more. I can't believe he did this."

It became clear that Gilbert was giving up on his brother. I was disappointed in Edwin too, but I wasn't going to give up on him, not now, not ever. Mother pretty much threw up her hands, pronouncing, "May it be God's will." Grandma whispered his name in her nightly prayers and entrusted him to *el angel guardian*. I was thankful for every day that passed without a disturbing phone call and continued to pray for a miracle that would turn his life around.

Edwin was out in less than a year and continued to roam the streets like a lost soul.

He and Anita met, as aimless spirits often do, on a dark squalid street where the hopeless gather in obscurity until the light of day infringes on their illusory existence. Edwin began to stay over at Anita's place, a disheveled fleapit in the projects, where Anita often left her two fatherless children alone while she cavorted in the streets, high as a kite.

Anita gave birth to Edwin's second child, a perfect little girl they named Kristy. Far from being the miracle that would change their lives, this beautiful child was tossed aside like the dirty laundry and discarded trash that littered their squalid hovel. That's how baby Kristy came to live at Mother's house.

Anita soon gave birth to Edwin's third child, Christian, whom she managed to carry to term while wasted on crack. It wasn't until a few years later that we discovered why Christian was failing to thrive. He was severely autistic.

Christian, too, came to live at Mother's house and soon became Bernadette's precious little boy. Knowing that they would not be able to adequately provide for their children, Anita and Edwin signed over their parental rights to my mother, and shortly after, Anita disappeared from their lives forever.

Eron and I managed to save enough money and bought a lovely two-story brick home on Seymour Avenue in the Bronx with an efficiency apartment in the basement It was everything I ever dreamed of, with front and back porches, a small garden at the entrance, and an above-ground pool. Located in the middle of a tree-lined street in a working class neighborhood, it was the perfect place to raise children and live a peaceful life.

14

Nightmare on Seymour Avenue

Our house was attached on one side to the Riveras' home, a very nice couple with two children. While the Riveras led an enviably tranquil and harmonious life, our arrival next door probably put a disquieting dent in their idyllic existence with our frequent, boisterous arguments. It was hard work interacting with them the next day and pretending that everything was just peachy between me and Eron.

"Isabel, come here and look at what José's doing," Eron called out to me one day. I looked out the window, and there was our neighbor chopping away at the lovely tall evergreen bushes that separated our entranceway from theirs.

"What on earth is he doing?" I asked.

"What does it look like he's doing? Those bushes are on our property, and he didn't even have the decency to ask us if we wanted them down!" Eron shouted as he turned towards the front door.

"Where are you going?"

"I'm going to tell him to stop!"

"Eron, please don't do that. It's no big deal. Please don't upset them."

"Upset them? Upset *them?*" The door slammed against the wall as he ran outside. Peering out the window, I watched the silent film motions of the two men making overt hand gestures, mouths moving in quick, overlapping succession. It would have been funny watching the scene had it not been a real-life drama. José won the argument, and the bushes were history.

On another occasion: "Isabel, come out here and look at this."

To the left of our house lived a friendly, peaceful Italian family whose home was separated from ours by a narrow, shared driveway. I went out to the porch to see what Eron was getting excited about. The Italians had spread huge barrels and some hoses across both driveways and were squashing tomatoes to make sauce. I thought it was so quaint and started to laugh.

"What the hell are you laughing at? Can't you see the mess they're making on our driveway? One of those hoses they're lugging around could dent my car. Oh, no! That crate of tomatoes he just carried out almost scratched my car. No, this has to stop," he said as he tore down the porch steps.

"Eron, please don't do that. Come back here," I yelled to deaf ears.

I went back inside the house and shut myself off from what might be transpiring outside. Who knew what connections these nice Italians had. I wanted no part of this disagreement.

A short while later, Eron entered the front door with two bottles of homemade spaghetti sauce and a sheepish grin on his face. Round two went to the Italians.

A very sweet young couple lived on the ground floor apartment, but no matter how tidy they were, Eron managed to find an issue to confront them. Eventually they got tired of the nitpicking and moved out.

Gilbert just happened to be looking for a place to start a new life with his fiancée, Shirley. I gently brought up the subject with Eron, even though I harbored some concerns about Eron's crabby attitude and how this would go down with my brother, who was not exactly a pushover.

"The apartment downstairs would be perfect for them. I think it would be great to have my brother and Shirley living there," I coaxed.

"I don't know about that. Having relatives live there might cause problems that we're not prepared to handle."

"Oh, Eron, what kind of problems do you think my brother could cause? They're both working, responsible adults, and I'd rather have them living there than perfect strangers who wouldn't give a damn about taking good care of the apartment," I said.

"I guess it would be all right," he finally said. I couldn't wait to tell Gilbert.

Eron finished his bachelor's degree and went on to study for the CPA exam while still working full time. I continued to work and do all the things that I was told were expected of a wife and mother. After work, I would take a one hour subway ride to the sitter's house, pick up Aimée. Then I'd take another one hour ride home on the bus, saddled with briefcase, bulky diaper bag, and a squirming child. It was especially tough in inclement weather. When Eron and I sat down to watch television after dinner, I'd be asleep by the time the first commercial break came on.

I was defining who I was in terms of the roles I believed I was expected to play. Who I was and who I had become were at odds and out of sync. My true self, that happy-go-lucky free spirit, was being stifled by the now ingrained expectations Eron and my culture had of me as wife and mother. The tendrils of unhappiness began to suffuse inside me, and without understanding my growing contempt, I forged ahead to super womanhood at the expense of my own sanity.

Eron was having his usual late night dinner when I quietly sat next to him, still trying to figure out the best way to tell him. There was no easy way.

"Eron...I'm pregnant."

"What?" He froze with his dinner fork suspended in midair and then abruptly let it fall on his plate. This was not exactly the reaction I expected. "What are you saying, Isabel? I thought you were protecting yourself?" he asked glaring at me.

"Well I was, but it's not the most reliable method. Accidents can happen, you know. Why are you so upset? I thought you'd be happy." I could feel the stinging of imminent tears.

"Happy? Isabel, we're under a lot of financial pressure right now. I still have my school expenses, and now we have a house to worry about. We can't afford to have another kid!" His voice kept rising with every word he uttered.

"Eron, our finances are not that critical! We can afford to have a baby."

"How would you know?"

I didn't know. Some time ago, Eron had decided my paycheck should go straight into the family pot, and he would hand me a stipend for travel, with a few extra dollars for my personal needs.

"I'm the one that takes care of the bills," he reminded me. "We have some money saved, but that's for emergencies. We can't have another kid now and that's that!" he said, picking up his fork again. I wanted to grab it and stick it in his face.

"What are you suggesting, Eron? That I have an abortion?" The tears came, more out of anger than hurt.

"I'm not suggesting anything. I'm telling you! Read my lips, Isabel. We can't afford a baby right now!" he said, enunciating every word.

"You bastard! It's so easy for you to make that decision. You don't have to go through it, I do! You could at least show some compassion!" I ran upstairs crying and slammed the bedroom door shut.

After a great deal of soul searching, I mentally prepared myself for this terrifying procedure by making myself believe it was for the best. What made it worst was that I couldn't share this with anyone. I felt so alone.

Eron drove me on a Saturday to a clinic where I terminated the pregnancy. It took me a long time to get over the loss and even longer to rid myself of the shame and guilt.

Eron's mother came to visit us for a month and, needless to say, I was not looking forward to it.

"*Ay Dios mio*, my back is killing me, and I have such a headache," she announced as she collapsed on the sofa. Here we go.

"Would you like some Tylenol or a cup of coffee?" I asked.

"Ay, no, I will have a sleepless night if I drink coffee now. I have some pills here that the doctor gave me," she said as she emptied a plastic bag full of medicine bottles.

I went to the kitchen and returned with a glass of ice cold water.

"Do you have any apple juice? I feel like drinking something sweet."

"No, but we do have orange juice," I said with a stiff smile.

"Ay, no, orange juice is too acid for me. Let me have the water then," she said. I made a mental note to get some apple juice and arsenic on my next trip to the supermarket.

Doña Edilia was kind enough to walk Aimée to school and back, but she complained about the walk, the weather, the traffic. After a long day at work, I dreaded coming home. Every night, I cooked dinner and served her wherever she sat and listened to a litany of ailments, woes, and what's wrong with the world.

"Eron, she complains constantly. I don't know how to deal with it. I try to change the conversation, but it always comes back to her moaning and groaning. And there's no pleasing her!"

"Isabel, just ignore her. She's always been that way, and there's no changing her. Just deal with it 'cause I'm getting tired of both of you complaining."

"What do you mean 'both of you'? She's been complaining about me?" I was stunned. What was there to complain about?

"She thinks you don't appreciate her. You know, she's doing us a great favor by babysitting Aimée. See if you can change your attitude towards her and maybe things will change." Then he added firmly, "Don't forget she's my mother, and you need to respect her."

"Eron, try to look at it from my point of view. I realize she's on vacation, but isn't it obvious that I could use a little help around here? I come home from a hard day's work to cook dinner and serve her hand and foot and listen to her complain. How about showing me some consideration?"

Suddenly, Doña Edilia appeared behind Eron. "I hear every word you say, and if you don't want me here, I leave."

She started to cry. "I don't want to cause you fighting. I will pack my bags and leave now."

"Now look what you've done!" yelled Eron, spit flying in my face. "You're just being a whiny bitch and you've upset my mother for no reason!"

"I am sick woman and there ees only little I can do," Doña Edilia sobbed. "You walk around with long face like I bother to you. Don't think I not notice," she complained.

"I have never disrespected you, but the truth is I work very hard, and I thought you were going to be of some help. Instead, you come here expecting to be served like I'm a maid!" I yelled over Eron's shoulder.

"Don't you dare talk to my mother like that, you bitch!" Eron yelled as he pushed me hard against the wall.

"That's the last time you're putting your hands on me, you bastard!" I ran upstairs, packed my bags, and was out the door with Aimée before anyone knew what was happening.

"Wait! Where the hell are you going? Come back here!" I heard Eron yell behind us, but there was no stopping me now.

I spent two days in my mother's house before Eron called and informed me that Doña Edilia was leaving the next day.

"Isabel, I know she can be very difficult, and I'm sorry that things had to go this way. I want you and Aimée home, where you belong," he said.

"Eron, give me some time to think about this. It's not just your mother. Things haven't been right between us for a long time, and I don't know if I can handle any more arguing and stress," I said.

"Isabel, you have to admit that I'm a good father and an excellent provider. I don't know what else you want from me. There are women out there whose husbands beat them and play them dirty all the time. Honestly, I really don't think that you could find a better husband than me, and you need to think about that."

"I hear you, but I don't think it's too much to ask that you show some appreciation for what I do and the support I've given you all these years. All I ever do is try to please you, but you show no recognition or gratitude," I said. I'd had this conversation countless times before, and it was getting old.

"Isabel," he said, his voice rising, "I don't mean to sound cold, but you do exactly what you're supposed to do. You do your part and I do mine, and that's the way it goes. Nobody at work thanks me for doing my job. Didn't your family teach you that your most important roles in life are as mother and wife? You should take pride in that."

"I would thank you to leave my family out of this. If I'd had a father who had the guts to stick around, maybe I would have learned something about roles. But I was raised by gutsy single women who taught me to be strong, and that's what I take pride in."

The following day, Eron showed up at Mother's house, begged and sweet-talked me into going home, and before I knew it, I was back where I started.

15

Panic and Pandemonium

It was late afternoon on a Friday when I made the shocking announcement to my dream team at the medical transcription program.

"As you know, the federal government has taken over the program and made changes that will change our recruitment and administrative policies. It was our unique strategy that made us the success we have been up to now, but all of that will change significantly as a result of their takeover. I'm afraid that I cannot condone or abide by these changes. I have come to the painful decision to hand in my resignation."

The faces staring back at me were frozen with mouths open. A silent pause allowed for their composure to thaw.

"Where are you going?"

"When are you leaving?"

"Who's taking over?"

"I have accepted a position as supervisor of the women's clinics at Mount Sinai Hospital. Jamal will be taking over, and I am confident that the program will continue to thrive under his capable hands."

I took a week off and started working at the hospital the following Monday.

My office was a ten by ten room which I shared with my supervisor, Susan, a twenty-something leggy yuppie with an icy cold personality to match her ghastly pale complexion. Cruella de Vil made it her mission to make my life a living hell.

"Where have you been? You're five minutes late. Put your things down and let's go. We have a meeting in ten minutes," she announced one day as I rushed into the lobby.

Eron and I had had a fight that morning, and as it was getting late, he drove me to work after dropping Aimée off at Susana's house. We continued the argument in the car, which became ever more heated with every traffic standstill. By the time I got to work, the sweat was pouring down my back, and my nerves were shot to hell. Now I had to face Cruella.

A couple of weeks before, Susan had received a phone call from her fiancé while she was out, and I took a message for her. Soon as she came in, I let her know Robert had called and he would try to call again later.

"Oh did he? Did you have a conversation with him?" she asked.

"No I didn't exactly have a conversation with him. I just..."

"What do you mean 'exactly'? Either you did or you didn't. What did you talk about?" she pressed on.

"We didn't talk about anything. He asked me if I was having a good day, and I told him I was, and then I asked him how his day was going, and he said it was okay, just the usual. He jokingly asked me if you were giving me a hard time, and I said no. I asked him if he wanted to leave you a message, and that's when he said he'd give you a ring later, and that was it." I took a deep breath.

"In the future, try and keep your conversations with my fiancé on a professional level," she said with icicles in her voice.

I didn't respond but made sure that I measured my words carefully when speaking to her from that day on. Obviously, Susan was precariously unhinged, and I needed my job.

Now I found myself taking brisk geisha steps trying to keep up with Susan's giant strides as we rushed towards the meeting room. It was empty when we got there. Punctuality was another of Susan's anal retentive peeves.

The meeting soon got underway at SRO capacity, with several bigwigs at the head of the table.

All of a sudden, I began to feel uncomfortably hot, and my thoughts began to race. The main speaker's mouth was moving, but I couldn't focus on what he was saying. Panic set in as I imagined people looking at me with sweat pouring down my face.

I have to get out of here! The compulsion to leave was overwhelming, but I was frozen in my chair and couldn't move. What is happening to me? I tried to slow down my thoughts and think rationally, to talk myself out of losing control. Somehow I managed to appear sane and blend in until the end of the meeting.

It happened again at a conference with Susan and another director. I could sense them glancing sideways at me while I squirmed in my seat. This time, I was able to excuse myself and run to the ladies room where I splashed cold water on my face and tried to regain my composure. Of course, Susan asked me what happened, and I gave her the excuse that I had the runs.

This was now becoming an embarrassment. The mere mention of a meeting would throw me into a tizzy, and I would come up with a myriad of excuses for not attending. It didn't always work.

The panic attacks didn't stop there. I started to get them when walking down hallways, crossing the street, or riding in the car with Eron. I got them on the subway platforms, where I would hang on to the steel columns for fear of losing my balance and somehow being blown onto the tracks.

The attacks would crop up in the most common situations, without rhyme or reason. They happened so frequently that I felt like I was in a constant state of panic, and my only safe haven was home. It became a living nightmare.

I went through several psychiatrists before I finally got help from a group that was doing research on panic disorder. With medication, I was able to sit through meetings and travel on the subways with moderate discomfort. But to this day, I cannot walk or drive across wide streets, even with medication. It has been a challenging stumbling block which has caused me great hardship, but when faced with a critical situation, I have always found a way.

The birth of my child had been a gift I readily accepted, and I treasured every moment with her. I wanted to share the miracle of childbearing with other women so that they too could experience the joys of giving life. I decided to join a natural childbirth women's group and become certified as a childbirth educator.

"What do you think about that?" I asked Eron one evening.

"Well, if you think you can manage a full time job, taking care of Aimée, and running a household, go for it," he said.

"It might be a little difficult, but maybe if you could watch Aimée while I take the classes..."

"That would be impossible, Isabel. I can't promise to be home at a certain time and my weekends are going to be spent studying for the CPA exam. There's no way I can study and watch her at the same time," he said.

"Eron, it would only be for a few hours on Saturdays. Once I'm certified, I could teach classes and make some extra money. I really want to do this."

"Well, if you can work out a system that doesn't involve me, like I said, go for it."

His objections became my challenge. I was going to do this whether he liked it or not, come hell or high water, and I was going to succeed.

Luckily, the participants were allowed to bring their babies to classes as long as we were able to keep them quiet during the lessons. Every Saturday, I packed a bag full of formula, food, and toys for Aimée, and with my baby strapped to me in a sling, I made the long haul on the train to Manhattan for my seminars.

It took a year and a half to get my certification. Afterwards, I was offered a job teaching natural childbirth classes at North Central Bronx Hospital in the evenings. I loved my work, but unfortunately, it required that Eron be home by six so that he could drive me there. He became resentful about having to be home by a certain time, and the unnerving arguments forced me to eventually quit.

I tried teaching classes at home, but that also became problematic when Aimee's needs imposed on Eron's study times. I was forced to give that up too. There was obviously no happy medium that we could live with for the moment, but maybe when Eron attained his CPA, things might change.

Just as Eron had predicted, our relationship with my brother and his new wife began to sour not long after they moved into the basement apartment. I could sense that Eron's controlling presence was a nuisance to Gilbert, and he and his wife pretty much kept to themselves. I was hoping that we could have a more amicable relationship. Unfortunately, Eron and Gilbert had nothing in common except for their strong-willed and stubborn characters, a winning combination for a potential display of fireworks under enough pressure.

To this day, I can't recall exactly what triggered the silence between Gilbert and me, nor will he discuss it, not even for the sake of filling in the gap in my memory. But one morning, Eron came to me and said, "Your brother just handed me his keys. They're leaving."

"What?" I felt like I had just been stunned with a Taser gun.

I rushed to the window and peeked past the closed blinds. Gilbert and Shirley were hauling the last of their belongings into a moving truck. He was leaving and taking my heart with him, for I could feel the pain of my soul being ripped out of me.

"Gilbert! Gilbert! Where are you going? Please don't go!" I screamed, banging on the windowpane. I rushed to the door, but Eron's voice stopped me in my tracks.

"Where are you going? You're not going out dressed like that," he said.

I realized I was still in my pajamas. "I have to talk to him. He can't do this!" I cried.

"Let them go. This would be a very bad time to talk to him. Wait a few days and then call him when everyone has calmed down."

"But he's going, Eron! My brother's leaving!"

"Let him go, Isabel! It's what he wants."

I went back to the window and sobbed uncontrollably as I watched the van pull away and my brother move out of my life.

A year of silence had transpired between my brother and me when I received a call from my sister Bernie.

"Isabel, Grandma's in the hospital."

"What's happened to her?" I asked, trying not to let my mind race to unspeakable thoughts.

"I don't know how else to tell you this. They found cancer in her bladder."

"Oh, no!"

"They're running tests on her because they think it spread," she said. "Isabel, we've decided not to tell her. We don't want to worry her or let her suffer more than she has already."

"I understand," I said. I went to work that day, unable to focus, getting through the day's order of business in a robotic state of detachment. I left Aimée at the sitter's for a few hours and hurried to the hospital to see my Grandma, *mi linda vieja.*

Sitting forlornly, staring out a window in a ward full of empty beds, Grandma seemed to have aged dramatically since I'd last seen her. She looked thin and fragile, her once radiant complexion now ashen and gaunt, her hair turned silvery white. The image of her sitting there alone against a bleak gray backdrop in the middle of a vacuous empty room was daunting.

I asked for her blessing as I gently embraced her lean shoulders. "*La bendicíon, Mamá.*"

"*Dios te bendiga mi'ja,*" she replied. God bless you, my child. I sat in a chair facing her and held her frail hands in mine. "How are your little one and your husband?" she asked.

"They're okay. I want to know how you're feeling, Mamá," I said, still fighting a losing effort not to cry.

"Ay, mi'ja, these doctors keep poking and testing, and I'm not getting any better." She paused and stared past me at the window. "I'm tired Isabel, and I'm ready to go. You children have your own lives now, and my work is done. I know I don't have much time left, and I don't want to be a burden to any of you. I'm ready to go."

"Mamá, please don't say that. You could never be a burden to us. You spent your whole life taking care of us, and now it's our turn," I said.

"No, Isabel. There comes a time when one has to accept one's fate, and I am ready. Don't be sad, Isabel. Someday we will all be together again."

"But Mamá, what will we do until then? I will miss you so much!" I reached out to her and held her as I cried inconsolably.

"Isabel, don't cry. I will always be with you. Always remember that."

I swiped away the tears and tried to control my emotions. There was so much I wanted to say to her. "Mamá...I just want to say...thank you for all you've done for us, for me. *Te quiero tanto.* I love you so much."

"I know you will never forget me," she said.

"No Mamá, I will never, ever forget you."

Life went on, and so did the silence between Gilbert and me. For whatever reason, neither of us dared to be the first to pick up the phone and break the disquieting barrier, though I was tempted many times. It was so much easier to just throw up our hands and walk away from it all, but in the process, we had lost each other.

In hindsight, it wasn't even worth it, the pain and loneliness we endured, the effect it had on the family. It never dawned on us that life is unpredictable, that one day, one of us could suddenly cease to exist, and what then? What would be the joy in having left so much unsaid? With what memories would we fill the empty silence?

Eron passed the CPA exam on his second try and was hired by a prestigious accounting firm in Manhattan. For me, matters carried on as usual. The only saving grace in my monotonous existence was Aimée. Now a precocious five-year-old with a dual personality, she could be happy and rambunctious one minute, and sensitive and whiny the next.

"Mom! Mooooom!" I'd hear her cry outside as she ran up the stairs. "Mom, Angela won't play with me!"

"Why not, sweetie?"

"I don't know. She said she only has two dolls, and she gave the other one to Emily, and now they won't play with meeee!" Oh, dear.

One day I left her playing in her room, and the prolonged silence became worrisome. I quietly went upstairs to see what she was up to.

"Aimée, what have you done!" She had cut her beautiful long hair so short on top, it was now standing up on end.

"Don't be angry, Momma. I want to look like Tina Turner. Can you fix it, Momma?" she asked with a pitiful look on her face. I laughed until my sides hurt.

Eron thankfully turned out to be an affectionate father who devoted quality time to little Aimée, when he had the time. On the occasional Sunday, we would pack a picnic bag and head out to Orchard Beach, Rye Playland or Central Park, where we could relax and watch Aimée play and have fun. It became my favorite pastime to watch her grow and learn and enjoy her childhood.

Just as my mother had done, I made sure that holidays and traditions were kept alive in my daughter's impressionable mind. But it was Grandma's uncompromising love for us that always served as my blueprint for raising my children.

I lasted two years working for the Borg Queen at the hospital before I finally decided I'd had enough. Dealing with bickering employees and boorish union reps made my decision that much easier. I went to work for a major insurance company without taking any time off.

It was a great job. I had a nice boss, worked on my own, not too much stress except for the commute to lower Manhattan. It was definitely a change for the better.

I had been working on some stats for one of our major clients when my supervisor suggested I could get more information from the claims department. Two floors down, I walked into a huge room with row upon row of workers sorting out claim forms.

"Holy shit!" yelled a tiny cocoa muffin from the middle of the room. She sprang from her chair as if she'd just won a game of bingo.

"Maria!" I shrieked as I ran to my childhood friend, crushing her with a mighty hug. The commotion made everyone stand in their tracks and stare. Talk about a small world. Countless questions overlapped as we excitedly exchanged tidbits of our lives.

"Oh, my God! How long has it been?" she asked.

"It's gotta be, what, seven or eight years?"

"I have a little girl now," she gushed as she grabbed a framed picture of her precious little one off her desk. "Her name is Jasmine."

"Maria, she's adorable! I have a little girl, too. I named her Aimée."

The lively chatter continued for another ten minutes before Maria noticed her supervisor giving her the evil eye. "Let's get together for lunch. I'll meet you in the cafeteria at 12:30," she said.

"I'll be there!"

We met for lunch where we filled in the spaces of time we had missed and traced the separate rocky paths we had taken. My best friend had returned, and I was overjoyed for now I had someone in whom I could confide. I wasted no time and told her all about Eron, the good and the bad.

"Oh no, girlfriend, you can't continue to allow him to control your life like that," Maria admonished.

"What life? I don't have a life."

"Exactly! Isabel, what is it costing you to be in this so-called marriage? If it's costing you your dreams, your spirit, or your dignity, then the price is too high. Suffering in silence isn't going to get it. You're becoming a martyr, and that's not the Isabel I know. Don't you realize that by not confronting him with his controlling ways, you are actually enabling him?"

"Maria, I've tried so many times to talk with him about the things that bother me, about my dreams and the things I'd like to do."

"Yeah, and...?"

"Well, he either tries to make me feel guilty by telling me that it's time I'm taking away from him and Aimée, or he gets very defensive, and we end up fighting."

"Isabel, he's a coward and a bully. He chooses to abuse the people who love him the most in a place where he feels safe and free to do so. I'll bet he doesn't act like this at work, where he knows he can get fired, or at a party, where someone he's just insulted might knock his teeth out."

"Oh I don't know about that, Maria. I think he's been lucky so far."

"Mira, if you're waiting for him to change, it's not gonna happen. You've already tried to have conversations with him, and he ain't listening. Now the one that needs to change is you," she said, pointing a finger at me. "If it was me, I'd tell him straight up—either loosen up or find the front door."

There was no need to soften the blow or make a flowery announcement. I knew what his reaction would be, and frankly, I didn't care. Aimée was now six years old, and it was time.

"Eron, I'm pregnant again."

"Really?" he asked as he continued to shovel food into his mouth.

"Yes, really. I went to the doctor today, and she confirmed that I'm twelve weeks pregnant."

"It's going to put a strain on our finances, but okay, great," he said, as if I was asking permission to buy another purse. "When is it due?"

"It's going to be my birthday present to you. It's due on your birthday, September 20. Isn't that fantastic?"

"That is fantastic!"

Once again, my changing body became a constant reminder that I was the gifted bearer of the consummate miracle. I felt blissfully content, at one with the life I was nurturing. My swelling girth and the fluttering movements inside me were cause for amusement and excitement as my baby's existence became ever more real.

I blew up like a Macy's helium-filled blimp, my legs swollen and painful. I continued to work and tackle the crammed subways and buses to get to Aimée and back home. Unbeknown to me, ignoring my symptoms was making my condition worse.

In my eighth month, Eron drove me to my next doctor's visit as getting around was getting increasingly difficult.

"Isabel, you have developed pre-eclampsia. I need you to go on complete bed rest for the duration of your pregnancy. We will need to monitor you and your baby closely, so please come in once a week for a check-up," stated my obstetrician with deep concern etched on her face.

"Doctor, is this absolutely necessary?" asked Eron. "Her work doesn't require that she stand for long periods and we can arrange…"

"Sir, perhaps I wasn't clear. Your wife's health and the health of your baby are at stake here. This condition can lead to seizures and, at its worse, to fetal or maternal demise. It's your decision, but personally, I wouldn't take any chances," she said sternly.

Eron decided to send for his mother so she could help out, a decision I accepted with mixed feelings. Since our heated argument a few years earlier, we had re-established communication via infrequent letters as Eron was too busy to write, and apparently, so was she.

Doña Edilia arrived a week later with her bags and the usual assortment of physical ailments. I now quietly hummed to myself whenever she griped.

My condition worsened, and I was consequently hospitalized for two weeks, until I spontaneously went into labor. Hoping that I could have my baby naturally, I held off for as long as I could before I finally told a nurse. Alarmed, she rushed me to the labor room in record time.

"You're only two centimeters dilated," announced the midwife. I couldn't believe it! All that pain, and I hadn't progressed. "Your husband is outside," she said. "I'll send him in."

Eron stood next to me, pale and disheveled. Déjà vu. Just when my stress level was about to give way to a torrent of vulgar expletives, three distinguished gentlemen in white coats came to see me. They asked Eron to leave.

"Isabel, we understand that you are not progressing, so we are going to puncture your amniotic sac. Hopefully this will help your labor move along." The minute he took that knitting hook and ruptured my sac, I felt the most excruciating contraction, its severity setting off a piercing scream at its greatest intensity. I had but seconds to get my breath back before another one struck.

An hour later, the three coats returned. "Your blood pressure is elevated and your baby is in distress. We need to do a Caesarean section immediately. I know you wanted a natural birth, but that is not an option. Your husband has been informed of the situation."

Although it was extremely uncomfortable getting an epidural from a resident in training, it was worth the torment to be able to experience the birth of my baby. When the time came, there was no fear, only joyful expectation and the innate feeling that everything was going to be all right, and it was.

We named our precious baby boy Daniel.

16

Life and Death

When my brother Gilbert and I stopped speaking to each other over a year before, the rest of the family did too, including Mother. So it was quite a shock when the door to my hospital room opened, and Mother walked in with a big smile and a lovely gift. She also brought her new beau, a younger man who apparently did wonders for her mindset and rosy appearance. It was good to see her again, happy and unruffled.

"Mami, what a surprise! You look wonderful!"

"How are you feeling?" she asked cheerfully, as if nothing had transpired between us.

"I feel terrific! It's so good to see you!"

"This is Arturo," she said. I greeted him warmly but was a bit put off by his youth. He appeared to be half her age.

"Come see my baby," I said as I rushed them out the door to the nursery.

Returning to my room, I finally got the courage to ask about Grandma. It had been several weeks since I'd last seen her, and the guilt of not having the courage to watch her deteriorate was eating me up inside.

"Grandma does not look well," she said with eyes downcast. It was the first time I saw my mother show sadness for Grandma's failing health. Where grandma's neediness may have once felt like an inconvenience to her, now it was becoming clear to Mother that Grandma's days were numbered.

At Mother's apartment, the tiny bedroom was crammed with medical supplies and other therapeutic paraphernalia. From the doorway, I could see the hospital bed, and in its center, a tiny mound curved in a fetal position beneath the blankets.

"Grandma?" I called to her.

Her eyes slowly opened, and there was instant recognition. "Isabel," she said, as her skeletal hand emerged from the covers and lightly touched my face. "The children?" she asked softly.

"Aimée is right here. I brought baby Daniel too."

"Let me see them," she said. I lifted Aimée, who gently kissed Grandma on her cheek. I then laid Daniel next to her. She encircled him with her arm and tenderly placed a kiss on his forehead. "God bless them," she said.

Her eyes closed, and she placidly returned to that space between here and there, where memories of bygone days become real, where those that have gone before us entice us to dance and sing and laugh again. I quietly left her with her reverie to face my own grief.

"Where are you going?" asked Eron.

"I thought I'd take the kids to visit Santa Claus at Macy's. Aimée could use a little holiday joy since you can't bring yourself to do anything with her lately."

"What the hell are you talking about now? I spend time with her! Are you in a bad mood again?" he asked indignantly.

"No, I wouldn't say that," I said as I picked up Daniel, who was bundled up to ward off the arctic weather. "Let's just say I'm annoyed that I have to think of everything, including trying to make a normal life for our kids."

"You're being a real bitch, you know that?" he yelled with fisted hands at his sides.

"And you're a cold, useless bastard! I'm sick of you!" I yelled back.

"Shut up! Just shut the hell up!" He pushed me, and I fell backwards onto the bed with Daniel still in my arms. Eron stormed out of the room, and a minute later, the front door slammed as he walked out.

"Momma, is Daddy coming back?" Aimée asked misty-eyed.

I felt ashamed that I had brought on this argument in front of her. "Yes, my little pumpernickel, he'll be back. But we're going out to see Santa, and it's going to be great fun," I said, trying to sound enthusiastic. I was not about to ruin the day for my baby.

"Yay!" she squealed, clapping her hands. Just then, the phone rang.

"Hello?"

"Isabel, it's Bernie."

"Hi Sis! What's up?"

"Grandma just died."

I screamed over and over as I fell to my knees.

How does one prepare for a moment like this, even when you know that your beloved has run out of time and miracles? Grandma—*mi viejita*. My source of light and love, my fountain of wisdom and inspiration, the paragon of all that is pure and good was gone.

I cried for that which I would miss most—her smile, her tender voice, her warm embrace, the love in her eyes. My children would grow never knowing this saintly woman the way I had known her.

"Momma?"

I don't know how long Aimée had stood beside me. Her little voice prompted me to regain my composure. My children needed me now.

"You remember what I told you about Grandma going to heaven?" I said as I dried my tears.

"Yes, Momma."

"Well, she left today, and I wasn't expecting it. It made me sad to hear that she'd gone, but I'm okay now, baby."

"Oh." After a pause, "Are we still going to see Santa Claus?" she asked.

Was it fair to expose her to more anguish? I wasn't exactly ready to face the family and the sadness either. Maybe this would give me the time I needed to pull myself together and be strong for them.

"Yes, let's go see Santa Claus."

At Mother's house, a shroud of grief veiled the once lively home whose inspiring spirit was now conspicuously gone. Mother threw her arms around me, and we both sobbed until our tears ran dry. Bernie and Mother's friend Letty were there, but Edwin and Wanda were noticeably missing. It was then that I saw Gilbert quietly walk from Grandma's room and sit on the sofa. I was at a loss as to what to do or say.

Abruptly, Letty grabbed my hand and dragged me into Grandma's old room. It was empty except for her old dresser, the shoddy portable TV where she watched her Spanish soap operas, and the antique rocking chair where she once sat and cuddled her beloved grandchildren.

"Wait here," she said. I could smell and feel Grandma's spirit in that room.

Seconds later, Letty appeared at the doorway, dragging my brother Gilbert behind her. "Shame on both of you for letting such a small thing come between you," she said. "It's time you two came together again. Do it for each other and for your grandmother. Your silence is probably breaking her heart," she said and walked out, leaving the two of us alone.

We both stood there with bowed heads, not daring to look into each other's eyes.

What should I say? What should I do?

The answer came to me in whispered words, like a quiet prayer in the night.

"Gilbert...I'm sorry. I'm so sorry this happened," I sobbed as I held out my arms.

"I'm sorry too, sis," he said as he came towards me. Our arms encircled each other in a powerful solidifying embrace.

"I missed you so much!" I cried.

"I missed you too, sis." He could barely get the words out.

"We must never let this happen again. Never will I let anything or anyone come between us. Never," I said. All he could do was nod as his pain and sorrow flowed freely in a deluge of tears.

As I held my brother, the ambiance turned into a surreal cloud of ambiguity as the present became the past, and my brother was nine years old again. Mother had beaten him until his stoicism was shattered and his tears flowed. "You wanna cry, you little bastard? Take this, and this," she'd say with each forceful blow.

"Stop it! Stop it! Stop hitting him!" I screamed as I yanked my brother away from her and shielded him in my arms.

But this time, it was me who had inflicted the pain. It was me who didn't have the guts to defend him and stand by him It was me who broke him and made him cry.

I held Gilbert for a long time, until his pain and my guilt dissipated in the aura of maternal love and forgiveness that still lingered in that room.

Grandma's viewing was held two days later at Ortiz's Funeral Home on Willis Avenue. Friends and family we had not seen in years came to say their final good-byes to this saintly woman who, in her humility and love for all, had touched so many.

I went outside to get a breath of fresh air and was pleasantly surprised to see Cousin Louie, who was standing by himself smoking a cigarette. His appearance had not changed since I last saw him. He looked forlorn and deep in thought.

"Hi Louie," I said as I hugged him. The smell of alcohol was unmistakable. "How long have you been standing here?"

"Oh, I've been here a while," he said, taking another puff.

"Why don't you go inside?"

He shook his head. "No, don't think I can."

There was a long pause as we both stared into the distance. Dusk had set in, turning the skies into horizontal shades of winter grays. A base of reddish gold peeked between the dilapidated buildings where the sun had disappeared.

People cowering against the frigid wind rushed past, their boots making sloshing sounds on the melted gray mush that covered the streets. Just outside the entrance, we could hear the murmur of hushed conversations and the whimpering of grieving relatives.

"Louie, what are you thinking?" I asked him, hoping he'd let go and bare his soul.

"Not much," he answered.

Time and distance had driven an irretrievable wedge between us and made us strangers. The memories of our childhoods together, of improvised games and lip-synched songs, of silly secrets and self-discovery had died long before Grandma did.

"Think I'd better go. It's getting late," he said, flicking his cigarette butt.

"Okay," I said and gave him a warm hug. "Take good care of yourself, Louie."

"You too," he answered as he waved good-bye and walked away.

Two days later, Louie was dead.

I received the devastating news from Bernie.

"Sis, Louie came by last night drunk. He was banging on the door, yelling 'I know you're in there! Open the door!' Mom told us to be quiet, and after a while, he went away. Then Uncle Anibal called this morning and told us. Isabel, he was murdered. His girlfriend got angry at him for some reason, and while he slept on the sofa, she stabbed him. He managed to get down the stairs and to the building's foyer. That's where his father found him."

"Oh, God, Uncle Anibal found him?"

"Yep," she said, with an almost matter-of-fact tone. "Uncle Anibal said he went to get some beer, and when he got back from the store, Louie was on the floor in the lobby. He thought Louie was drunk, but when he turned him over, he saw the blood. It's terrible, Isabel. He died in his father's arms."

The day after Grandma's burial, I attended Louie's funeral service. Uncle Anibal, unkempt and unshaven, his face contorted in a mask of grief, reeked of alcohol. We embraced, both of us sobbing unabashedly.

I didn't go to Louie's burial. On that day, I took a long walk alone as a feather-light flurry of snow fell. The distant sound of children's laughter blended into flashbacks of snowball fights and sand castles, of games of make-believe and hide-and-seek in a tiny apartment.

The timing of Louie's death raised so many questions about life and death and the ironies of fate. But the answers were as elusive as the delicate snowflakes that swirled from the muted gray skies and vanished on the concrete pavement

17

Omens and Fate

E ron and I were watching TV one night when the door-bell rang. Standing in the doorway was a smiling mid-dle-aged couple.

"Hello," said the gentleman. "We heard from one of your neighbors that you're selling your house, and we were inter-ested in getting more information."

Eron and I looked at each other in disbelief. We had been thinking of moving to the suburbs but hadn't discussed any details. I let Eron take the lead.

"Well, we hadn't made any plans to sell just yet, but I'd be happy to show you around," he told them. We both shrugged our shoulders. What the heck. They didn't look like home invaders or nut cases.

Eron gave them a tour of the house while I attended to the children. When they were finished, I overheard the man tell Eron, "We are very interested, so give us a call as soon as you come up with a price." He handed Eron his business card and thanked him profusely for his time.

"Eron, this is very strange. What are we going to do?"

"Well, they seemed very motivated. Let's make them a ridiculous offer and see where it goes. We could make a killing with the right price," he said.

After some discussion, Eron decided to set the sale price at double what we had originally paid for the house. It was an outrageous amount, and I had a feeling that the nice couple would think it laughable.

The next night, Eron called the couple back and gave them the sale price.

"You're not going to believe this, Isabel. He accepted our offer, just like that!"

"This is incredible! But what are we going to do? Where are we going to live now?" The news was exciting but frightening. There were so many things to think about, so many plans to make.

"How about we get a map and throw a dart?" he asked.

"Not a good idea. What if it lands in a swamp or a desert?"

"If that's where we're led, then that's where we'll go," he said with a silly grin.

"I don't think so," I said.

"The smart thing to do would be to move someplace where we could buy a house outright and maybe have some money left over. Imagine not having a mortgage!" he said. I could see the dollar signs roll in his eyes.

"How about looking outside of New York?" I suggested. "Someplace quiet with less traffic and noise and where housing prices aren't so high? I'm really tired of living here, and the traveling from the babysitters every day and the cold weather."

Suddenly I got an idea. "You know, Gilbert's father lives in Florida. How about we give him a call and get some information from him?"

"You think we could call him now?" he asked.

"I don't see why not. Let me give Gil a call and get his father's number in Florida."

That evening, we had a lengthy conversation with Gil senior. The more we talked, the more excited we got about moving to Florida. It just seemed so right.

Gilberto offered a suggestion. "The best thing for you to do is to call a realtor or builder and ask questions. I'll give you the number of the main one where I live. You can start there."

After that conversation, everything happened so fast, it all seemed like a blur. Eron flew to Orlando the following week and met with a realtor. New homes were being built in a rapidly growing town just south of Orlando, and the sale prices were unbelievably affordable.

After a few days of house hunting in Florida, Eron called me with great news. "Isabel, we just bought a house! It's still being built, but I saw pictures of it, and it's perfect," he said. "It's huge and will have a great backyard for the kids. It's near schools and shopping centers, but you would have to learn how to drive to get to them. Everything here is so different. Get this—the elementary school that Aimée will attend is called Boggy Creek Elementary."

"Boggy Creek? Eron, where did you buy this house, in a swamp?" Images of alligators and marsh creatures hanging around the school's playground came to mind.

"Oh yeah, did I tell you the house is on stilts? Don't be silly! Isabel, wait till you see how beautiful it is out here—lots of space and trees—and the weather is fantastic!"

"Okay, when can we move?" I asked.

"Soon as I get home, we're packing our bags."

Oddly enough, my department at the insurance company was being relocated to Connecticut in a bid to save on space rental in Manhattan. I had been in a tizzy deciding whether to commute to Connecticut or take their severance package and move on to something else. The choice was made clear.

Once again, I found myself questioning fate or if events do happen by chance and circumstance. What was the meaning behind this sudden upheaval? When a seemingly inexplicable event occurs in our lives, is it merely coincidence, or is there rhyme and reason behind the confusion?

We were in the midst of packing, the house in complete disarray, when Lucky, my saucy ex-pupil and now good friend, decided to pay me a final visit. Eron was in one of his stressed-out, pissed moods, which was quite obvious to my good friend, much to my embarrassment. She said nothing, but I could tell that she was very concerned. I led Lucky upstairs to a bedroom where we could talk privately.

"I'm so sorry, Lucky. He's a bit..."

"There's no reason to apologize. I understand. I'm going to leave now, but I want you to know that I will always be thinking of you, and I'm going to pray that everything works out for you," she said.

There was an understood finality in our parting. No need to lie and make promises we weren't going to keep. I hugged her and started to cry. "Don't cry, baby," she said. "We're both going to be okay. Life has dealt us some bad hands, but they have made us stronger, and there's little we can't handle. Keep your chin up and stay strong. Remember I love you."

"I'll never forget you," I said hugging her again. I was having trouble letting go and with good reason. It would be the last time I'd ever see my friend.

We had shipped our belongings by moving van, and now Eron, the kids, and I were on our way to Florida. To save money, he decided to drive there nonstop except for the obligatory bathroom breaks. We were all miserable and cranky by the time we reached our destination twenty-two hours later.

We moved into our spacious new home and got busy settling in. Eron began job hunting and teaching me to drive. I was a nervous wreck at the wheel, and once I managed to drive at twenty-five miles an hour, Eron decided I was ready to take the driver's test. As the test did not require driving on busy roads, I was able to pass it by the skin of my teeth.

Driving in an empty parking lot was one thing, but driving on open roads brought on the dreaded panic attacks full blast. I had no choice but to train myself to overcome them. Every morning, I'd get up at 5:00 a.m., and while the roads were still relatively empty, I would practice driving until I could get to a speed that wouldn't annoy other drivers.

Life resumed at a level near normalcy as we quickly became acclimated to our new surroundings. Eron got a job as an accountant in a firm located over an hour's drive away from home. I started to babysit from home but got no personal satisfaction from it and soon became bored.

Less than a year later, Eron began to gripe about his long, stressful commute to work.

"Why don't you take some money from our savings and open up your own accounting business?" I suggested.

Within a month, Eron was running his own accounting service from a beautiful office downtown. I got great satisfaction out of helping him put it all together—shopping for furnishings and supplies, advertising, and establishing a base clientele. It was a very exciting and promising venture.

Having accomplished that, I went on to look for a job and was hired in the medical records department of a local hospital. My supervisor, Cindy, was a pint-sized paragon of southern charm and goodwill. In her fifties, Cindy's short brown hair and sparkling blue eyes were the adornments of a plumpish figure that she dressed stylishly, every hair in place, makeup applied flawlessly. Her sugar-coated Dixie drawl dripped with sweetness. I felt very lucky.

"Mom, Desiree invited me to the water park tomorrow. She wants me to sleep over. Can I go?" asked my spunky eight-year-old.

"Which one of you is driving?"

"Oh, Mom, her mother's driving!"

"Oh, so there's a parent involved."

"Of course!" she said, hand on hip.

"What's her mom like? Have you met her? What does she do for a living, and where do they live?" I wanted to know.

"Her mom is really nice. She's a teacher at our school," she said, opening the refrigerator and perusing the goodies.

"Oh, that's cool. So, are there any men in the house?"

"Nope," she said, grabbing a Popsicle. "Her mom and dad are divorced."

"Does she have any brothers or sisters? And put that back. It's almost dinnertime."

"Crap!" she said under her breath. "No, no brothers or sisters. Just her and her mom."

"Sounds okay. And watch your mouth, young lady!"

From the moment I met Desiree's mom, Evelyn, she and I hit it off like two long-lost sisters. Caring, outgoing, and a great listener, she became a depository for my secrets and sappy rantings.

"You know what the jerk did today?" I said to her in one of our blab sessions over the phone.

"Oh, God, what now?" she asked.

"Remember I told you that last month he joined a gym?"

"Yeah...?"

"Well today he showed up with...hold on to your girdle...a brand new car!"

"Are you kidding me?"

"Not just a brand new car, but one of those sporty ones with leather bucket seats and fancy gadgets that light up on the console. Meantime, I'm driving around in a used tin carcass with wheels. Can you believe that, Evelyn?"

"Isabel, there's something wrong with this picture. It sounds to me like he's having a midlife crisis. You know what comes next, don't you?" she asked.

"What?"

"*Los cuernos salen.* The affair happens. My ex-husband had an affair. Actually he had a few. I forgave him the first time, but when he kept doing it, I told him to pack his bags and leave. It hurt like hell 'cause I still loved him, but I couldn't trust him anymore. I couldn't stand not knowing where he was and wondering if he was with another woman. Isabel, do you think Eron's having an affair?" she asked.

"I don't think so, but I can't say for sure. You know what, Evelyn? I don't think I care. He makes me feel so worthless, so unattractive. He's been on my case about my weight, and I haven't gained that much for him to be so blah. Maybe he is having an affair, but I don't see how. I always know where he is."

"Wake up, girl! When he tells you he's going to check Pedro's balance sheet, are you sure he's not checking out Petra's inventory?" she asked.

"No, I don't know that for sure," I said laughing. "But I really doubt it. I'll just play it by ear and keep my eyes open."

"You do that," she said.

"Isabel, we need to talk," Eron said one evening, lighting up his weed. Even in no-man's land, Eron would find a pot peddler.

"Okay," I said apprehensively, wondering what this was all about.

"I'm not happy here, Isabel. I'm not making enough money from the business, and this place is boring and backwards. I miss New York. I don't feel like I have anything in common with anyone here," he said, visibly frustrated.

"Eron, I miss my friends and family too, but we're settled here. Aimée's happy in her school, Daniel's doing well in daycare, and I have a great job. Look at this beautiful home we have. We could never get anything like this in New York for the same price," I reasoned. "Would you like to try getting another job, maybe?"

"No, I don't want to do that. It's more than just the job. It's this place. I don't like anything about it except maybe the weather. I want to go back to New York," he said adamantly.

"Obviously you've already thought about this and made up your mind. It doesn't sound like my opinion is necessary."

"I don't need your drama right now," he said with a hint of anger. "I've thought about what's best for all of us. This place is primitive, and we are never going to grow here. No, I've made up my mind, and you do have a choice. You can stay here with the kids or come back with me."

"Isabel, what are you going to do?" asked Evelyn.

"What can I do? I can't deprive the kids of their father, and I honestly don't think I can make it out here on my own. I have no one here, Evelyn."

"You have me!" she said. "Isabel, this is your chance to get out and be your own woman. You can do anything you want without him around telling you how to live your life and making you miserable. You can be free, Isabel! Look at me. I'm a single parent. It was hard at first, but as you can see, it didn't kill me to be without my husband. Now I love my freedom, and if I meet someone, fine. If I don't, that's okay too."

"I can't think like that right now. We've been together for fifteen years. That's a long time, and I just can't see myself starting over at my age and with two kids. Maybe when we go back to New York, he'll be happier and things will change. Who knows?" I rationalized.

"Oh, Isabel..." she said, shaking her head.

18

Betrayal

E ron decided to go to New York and find a job and a place for us to live, while I stayed in Florida to find a buyer for the house.

Although I loved New York, and a part of me will always be there, I hated the idea of rejoining the rat race—back to the daily grind of work, taking subways, finding babysitters, and enduring the cold weather. I resigned myself to my lot and moved forward to the day when we could join Eron and start over.

He came home that Christmas a different man. He was distant and uncommunicative, going through the motions of sharing in holiday activities without any holiday spirit. "I'm just tired and stressed out," he'd say by way of apology.

He had been in New York three months when he decided to move out of his friend's place and into a studio apartment, explaining that it was a temporary arrangement until a bigger apartment became available.

Late one Friday evening, I gathered Daniel, now a sprite four-year-old, and Aimée, my sassy ten-year-old.

"Let's surprise Daddy and give him a call. I'll turn on the intercom so we can all talk to him."

"Okay," they cheerfully said in unison. I dialed the number for them.

"Hello?" said the voice on the other end... a woman's voice.

"Oh...I'm sorry," I said flustered. "I have the wrong number," and hung up. "Sorry, kids. Let's try that again." I carefully redialed the number, making sure I hit the right buttons.

"Hello?" It was the same woman's voice.

This can't be right, I thought. Why would there be a woman in Eron's apartment at this time of the night? Instinctively, I turned off the intercom and picked up the receiver.

"Can I speak to Eron, please?" I managed to calmly get the question out in spite of the lump stuck in my throat.

"Who's this?" she asked.

"A friend," I said.

I heard a clicking sound, as if the woman was hitting the phone hook to disconnect. I heard her say, "Eron, the phone won't disconnect!"

"Just hang up the receiver!" Eron shouted. The phone went dead.

I don't know how long I sat there frozen with the receiver in my hand. In shock, my perception hovered over a fine line between reality and delusion. *This can't be!*

After putting the kids to bed, I called my sister Wanda in New York. Briefly, I told her what had just happened and asked her to get me the number of a twenty-four-hour private investigator.

I dialed the number she gave me, and a gentleman explained their fees and the services they offered. The investigator informed me that they could only confirm who was in the apartment for the amount I was able to afford. Photos would be extra.

"I just want to know who's in there," I told him.

I sat at the kitchen table surrounded by a deafening silence, still frozen, unfeeling. Lucidity began to painfully emerge as time passed. Maybe there was an explanation for this. Maybe it's a co-worker or a family member I don't know. Maybe...

The phone rang, and I quickly picked it up. "Isabel?" It was the investigator.

"Yes?"

"I sent one of my men over to the location you gave me. He confirmed that there was a male and a female in the apartment. There was Spanish music in the background so he couldn't make out exactly what was being said. Are you interested in getting photographs?"

"No, no...." I hung up the phone. "No...no!"

I screamed until exhaustion dropped me to my knees, my head pounding with my cries of denial still resounding. The pain was so unbearable, it became physical. I walked over to the medicine cabinet and took out my bottle of anxiety pills.

Sitting at the kitchen table, I popped one, then a second and a third. I just wanted the pain to go away.

The phone rang. I picked it up thinking it was Eron.

"Isabel?" I recognized the voice of Gilbert's wife. Shirley. Funny she should be calling at this hour, I thought.

I felt lightheaded and very calm. Everything was happening in slow motion.

"Hi Shirley. How are you?" The words flowed listlessly like a flurry of soap bubbles.

"Isabel, what's wrong? You sound kinda funny. Is everything all right?"

"No, Shirl, everything's not all right. I just found out...Eron's with another woman. He's with someone else, Shirley."

"Isabel, what have you done? Why do you sound so groggy? Where are the kids?"

"No, no, don't worry. They're here, sleeping. I just took a couple of pills...to calm me down. I'll call you tomorrow. I just want to... to sleep now. Tell my brother I love him. I'll be all right. Everything's going to be all right. I just want to sleep."

"Isabel? Isabel, wait..."

"Good night, Shirl. Talk tomorrow." I hung up the phone, put my head down on the kitchen table, and passed out.

I sluggishly awoke to a commotion outside. Flashing lights shone through my window. Someone was banging on my door and calling my name. Slowly I made it to the door and opened it. Men in uniform, lots of them.

"What do you want?"

"We got a call from your brother who's worried about you." The uniform spoke into his phone. "We're here, Gilbert. She seems to be okay. We'll call you back in a few minutes." Turning to me, "What's going on here? Anyone else in the house?"

"My kids." My brain was mush. Thoughts came in spurts. Nothing was real. I just wanted to be left alone.

I found myself sitting at the kitchen table. A different uniform picked up my bottle of pills.

"How many of these have you taken?"

"Just a couple," I said.

"M'am, we need to take you to the hospital and get you checked out. Is there anyone who can take your children for a few days?"

"There's nothing wrong with me. I'm okay. Just leave me alone."

"No, m'am, you need to go with us now. Who can we call?"

"My friend Evelyn. Call Evelyn."

"No, we need a family member. Do you have any family we can call?"

"No, I have no family here."

"M'am, if you can't come up with a family member, we'll have to take the kids into temporary foster care until you're released."

"No, no, you can't do that! You can't take my kids! I won't let you!"

"We can and we will unless you can come up with some-one other than a friend," he said.

Why are they doing this? Think, Isabel, think. "My supervisor. Will you let them go with my supervisor?"

"What's her name and phone number?"

"Cindy. Her name's Cindy. Her number is on the refrigerator."

It seemed like just minutes had passed before Cindy arrived. One of the officers spoke with her in a hushed voice.

"Oh, my!" Cindy said in her gentle drawl. "Isabel, it's best if you go with them. Where are Aimée and Daniel?"

"Sleeping. Cindy, I'm so sorry. I didn't mean for this to happen."

"No, honey, don't you cry now. It couldn't be helped. Now you go and git yourself better and I'll stay here with the children until you git back. They'll be fine, you hear?"

I was taken to the hospital where I was checked over and then transported to a psych unit.

By the next morning, I was clearheaded and rational. All I could think about was getting back to my children. They must be so scared and worried, I thought.

I sat smoking a cigarette in the lounge when a nurse approached me. "Isabel, you have a phone call. It's your husband. Do you feel up to talking to him or do you want me to give him a message?"

Did I want to hear what he had to say? What could he say but that he was sorry? He had a lot of explaining to do before I could even begin to forgive him. I decided to take the call.

"Isabel?"

"What do you want?"

"How are you?"

A stupid question like that did not deserve an answer. "How did you find me?" I asked.

"Your brother called me and told me what happened. I called the hospital, and they told me you'd been transferred out, but they wouldn't tell me where. So I just called around until I found this place. Isabel...I'm really sorry," he said.

"You damn well should be. Have you any idea what this has done to me and our children? It's going to take me a long time to forgive you and even longer to forget, you bastard!"

"Isabel...there's no easy way to say this. I've found some-one I want to be with. The truth is, I don't love you any-more. I stopped loving you a long time ago. I think we should talk about ending this."

"You filthy son-of-a-bitch! You called me here to tell me this!"

"I know you're angry, and I can understand it. If you want to talk about it later..."

I slammed down the receiver. My knees buckled, and I collapsed into a pathetic heap of broken dreams and bitter regrets.

They gave me my discharge papers that afternoon after I convinced a counselor that I was not suicidal and that I needed to be with my children. I was glad to be home, but now I had the daunting task of facing my children's tough questions.

"Momma, is Daddy coming back?" asked Aimée.

"I'm not sure, baby."

"Why does he want to stay away, Momma? Doesn't he love us anymore?"

"It's not that, sweetie. Apparently he's found another woman who makes him happier than I could. His choice to leave has nothing to do with anything you or Daniel did. I want you to remember that."

"Is he going to kiss her?" asked Daniel.

"I suppose he will, you silly boy," I said laughing, trying not to focus on the thought.

"What's going to happen now?" Aimée asked with deep concern.

"Well, hopefully he'll stay in touch with you. I want you both to know that I love you very much, and even though your dad may not be with us, I will never leave you. I will always be here for you no matter what." I scooped them both in my arms and bear-hugged them. "Now go put on your 'jamas and get to bed. You have school tomorrow."

"Yes, Momma!"

I sat at my kitchen table, chain smoking and drinking cup after cup of coffee. I felt so alone, so dejected. The emptiness he left behind wasn't just in the house—it was inside me, echoing through every thought. It all felt like some twisted dream, too cruel to be real, too strange to trust my own memory. I found myself reaching for the phone, desperate to hear his voice, to understand *why*. What was he thinking when he walked away?

I picked up the phone and dialed his number.

"Hello?" he answered. I could hear salsa music playing in the background.

"Eron, we need to talk. I think you're making a big mistake and we should talk this through."

"No, Isabel. I've made up my mind. I want to go on with my life, and you need to get on with yours."

"Eron, how can you just give up on us after all we've accomplished together? What about the kids? Have you thought about what this will do to them? Isn't that alone worth thinking about?"

"I've thought about them, and I'm really sorry to put them through this, but I can't be a good father to them if I'm not happy, and I'm not happy with you, Isabel. Please get that through your head."

"Eron, please don't do this. At least tell me you'll think about it. This has happened too fast, and I'm having a really hard time coping with this. I need your help to get through this. Don't just turn your back on me and leave me to deal with this by myself. Please don't do this!"

At that moment, I heard the woman's voice in the background. "You want to help her? Don't talk to her anymore!"

"Isabel, there's really nothing else to say. I need to hang up now," Eron said.

"No, Eron, please wait!"

"Hang up on her, *puñeta!*" the woman yelled. I heard the click and the line was disconnected.

"Please don't do this! Don't do this!" I cried into the phone's dead silence.

Out of control, I spiraled down a dark abyss, my screams echoing against its distant walls.

Don't do this. Please don't do this.

Free falling, nothing to grab onto. The sickening force of gravity rammed my guts into my throat. I couldn't breathe. I was screaming, but no sound came forth. No one could hear me.

Familiar voices whispered poisonous words. I pressed my hands against my ears, but the voices were inside my head.

You're not good enough.

Go with him then, you whore, and don't you dare call or write.

I can fool her but not you.

I just don't love you anymore.

My body hit rock bottom and crashed into water. I was drowning, arms flailing, struggling to rise to the top. I sensed my spirit draining from me, dying. I gave in. What will be, will be. Easier to give in than to fight. I floated peacefully towards nothingness.

I heard the distant sound of a phone ringing. Suddenly, I was grasped by an invisible hand and forcefully pulled straight up, out of the tranquil waters. I sat bolt upright in my bed, drenched in sweat. The clock next to my ringing phone read 2:30 a.m.

"Hello," I answered in a raspy voice.

"Hello," said the female on the other end. "You know who this is, don't you? I'm surprised you're still around. Weren't you going to kill yourself?"

I hung up, turned off the ringer and answering machine, and waited for daylight to come.

A few days later, I received another call. "Hello," she said cheerfully, "guess who this is. It's Marla, your husband's fiancée. He just bought me a gorgeous diamond engagement ring, and he paid $2,600 for it. You should see it."

I hung up and changed my number.

"Hi, Evelyn. It's me. Can you come over? I need you."

"I'll be right there," she said. Within fifteen minutes, she was at my door.

"Evelyn, I can't stand the pain anymore. It's too much too fast. I just can't handle it."

"I know this is very hard for you, Isabel. I went through this too but at least my husband was more sympathetic. He knew he did wrong, and he was the one begging me to come back. But I'd been down that road before with him, and I just couldn't trust him anymore." After a pause, "What would make it easier for you to accept this, Isabel?"

"I just can't believe that he's thought this through rationally. I think that woman has him by the cojones and won't let go. If only I could talk to him alone, face-to-face, maybe it would become more real to him," I said. "This might sound crazy to you, but I feel like going to New York and knocking some sense into him."

"Hmm, I've got mixed feelings about that. What if he still decides to stay with her? Could you handle that?" she asked.

"Evelyn, if he can look me in the eyes and tell me that he wants to be with her, then I'm done."

"Okay then, let's do it!"

The following day, I called Eron at work. "Eron, I'm going to New York tomorrow, and I need you to pick me up. We need to talk," I said.

"I don't think that's a good idea, Isabel. Why can't you just leave it alone?"

"Eron, I think after fifteen years of marriage and all that I've put into it, I deserve to be heard. Just give me a few minutes of your time to talk this through. If you still decide that you don't want to be with me, then I'll leave."

After a long pause, he said, "Okay, fine. What time does your flight get in?"

JFK terminal was bustling with hordes of commuters rushing in different directions like carpenter ants on a mission. A chance break in the crowd brought into view the man whose heart I had come to recapture. Barely recognizable in shabby clothes, with sunken eyes and unshaven, Eron's appearance evinced a broken man. We simply said hi to each other and walked silently to his car.

"I don't know why you had to come here," he finally said as he lit up a reefer.

"I came here because I thought it was worth it to save our marriage. This has happened too fast for me to feel satisfied that you know what you're doing," I said.

"Isabel, I thought I knew what I was doing. Now I feel so confused." Silent tears began to flow down his face. I decided to remain quiet and let him talk, but he said nothing and continued to cry until we got to his apartment.

As soon as we got through the door, the phone began to ring. He didn't answer it. We both knew who it was.

"Eron, what happened to us? When did this all go wrong?" I asked, trying desperately to understand.

"I don't want to hurt you, Isabel. But if you want to know the truth, I think I stopped loving you a long time ago. You started to gain weight, and I didn't feel attracted to you anymore. This girl I met, she's ten years younger than me. She's very attractive, and when she started to show interest in me, I felt like a man again."

The phone started to ring again.

"That is very painful to hear. Did you ever stop to think that every line and scar, every imperfection you turn away from are the price I paid for the children I bore for you. I wish you had told me how you felt."

"I did try to tell you, so many times," he said, taking a drag on his second joint.

The phone rang again, but this time, he answered it. He spoke to her softly, giving short cryptic replies.

"Why did you answer that?" I wanted to know.

"She knows that you're here, and she's just worried. I was talking her out of coming over," he said.

"I just flew 1,000 miles to be here and talk with you. The least you can do is respect that and give me a little of your time."

"I didn't ask you to come here, Isabel. As a matter of fact, I asked you to give me some space so I could think this through."

"And I did what I thought was fair—to give myself the opportunity to speak with you alone and be heard."

"Isabel, I think I'm in love with this girl, and I don't feel anything for you. I think it's best if you get on with your life and forget about me. I'm really sorry to put you through this, but that's how I feel," he said.

The finality of it all became crystal clear. I had my answer. I called for a cab and gave the dispatcher my brother's address as my destination.

Standing by the door, I gave it one last try. "Think about what we've been through together. Think about Aimée and Daniel. Is she worth their pain?" We were both crying now.

"I'm so sorry, Isabel. Come here," he said as he reached out for me.

"No, don't touch me. If this is good-bye, then let me go. Guess I won't be needing this," I said as I took off my wedding band and threw it at him.

"Isabel, wait…" I heard him shout as I flew out the door.

Gilbert and Shirley were surprised to see me standing at their door, bag in hand and cheeks streaked with mascara. They patiently listened as I shared the sordid details of my failed plan.

Gil said, "I wish you had told me that you were going to do this. I would have gone to the airport myself and turned your ass right around." My brother has never been one to mince words.

"I'm so scared of being on my own with two kids, and I worry about what this will do to them."

My brother, in his infinite wisdom said, "Why don't you just pretend that the asshole dropped dead? You can't call or write to a dead man. Put a couple of candles in front of his picture, say a few Hail Marys, and get it over with."

"Ignore him," said Shirley.

"He's been such a jerk all these years. Why would you want to stay with him?" asked Gilbert.

"We've had some good times," I said defensively.

"I don't get it. Some guys treat you females like shit, and when he finally decides to leave, all you can remember is the good times? Then start remembering the bad times and get a reality check," he said.

"I hate to say this, but he's kind of right, Isabel," said Shirley.

"Not 'kind of.' I *am* right," Gil retorted.

"As far as the children are concerned, do you think they'd be happier watching you and Eron fight all the time or would they feel more comfortable living with you in a peaceful home?" asked Shirley.

"Okay, okay, you guys have made some good points. I've got a lot to think about."

"Great!" said Gil. Turning to Shirley, "Now bring out that disgusting cheesecake you bought yesterday and let's get rid of it!"

Back in Florida, I made a conscientious effort to maintain some semblance of normalcy for my children, facing the day with stoicism and crumbling into despondency under the shroud of darkness.

That summer, in desperate need of a diversion from the humdrum routine of life, the kids and I traveled to New York. Mother was well aware of my marital problems though we didn't discuss them in any great detail. But one day she said to me, "Isabel, I want to take you to see a lady I know, a spiritualist. She is very good. Maybe she can help you."

I wasn't opposed to any kind of guidance, even if it was from an otherworldly source.

She took me to the third floor of a rundown project in the South Bronx. We knocked on a dented metal door which was opened by a dark-skinned young man. He said nothing but stepped aside and solemnly gestured for us to come in.

Sitting in the cramped living room were at least a dozen people, all of whom sized us up as we walked in. The space was cluttered with knickknacks, plastic flowers, and assorted photos, offering no insight into the gifted oracle except for the mixed scents of incense and cigar smoke. I had no idea what to expect.

It didn't take long for my mother to spark a conversation with those present, which provided a welcome respite from the long, tedious wait.

Two hours later, I was silently ushered into a bedroom by the same young man who had opened the door.

"Come in, my child, come in," she said in Spanish. "I have been expecting you."

Sitting in a rocking chair was a huge Black woman dressed like Aunt Jemima, puffing on a cigar. Rows of colorful beads hung from her stodgy neck. Next to her was a tall shrine adorned with statues and photos of saints, flowers, incense holders, and a glass of water. An array of large candles and tea lights provided the only illumination in the room.

"I know why you come. There is no need to be afraid. I am here to help you."

At once, I felt an overwhelming sense of reverence, for the lady appeared infinitely all-knowing and powerful.

There was something striking about her Spanish dialect, a distinctive Afro-Creole blend. She offered an incantation to her Lukumi ancestors while I looked on mesmerized. Then she began to speak.

"There is an evil woman who has blinded your husband and dropped a veil of tears over you so that you cannot see the truth for what it is. What you need to know, my child, is that she has done you a great favor. Let him go for they deserve each other. You were not happy with him. Why do you insist on distorting the truth?"

I was taken aback by this simple revelation.

"That house you live in, it is no longer a home. You must leave there and find your happiness. It is filled with dark memories and sorrow," she said. "Your husband is very confused and in his confusion has chosen a dark path. Do not allow his confusion to become yours. It will bring nothing but more misery for you and your children. Leave at once. Then you will find true happiness."

"Yes, señora. I am listening."

"Before you leave, I will try to lift that veil of deception, but you must also help yourself, mi'ja."

She stood and began to blow cigar smoke all around me. She then took a small broom and lightly whisked my shoulders and my back while chanting an incantation in a primitive language I did not understand.

"Go now in peace, my child, and may God bless you."

My co-worker Millie and I were having our morning rolls and coffee when the phone rang. I answered with the requisite office greeting.

"Isabel…. it's Eron. Can you talk?"

Caught off guard, I was at a loss for words. Our divorce was almost finalized after drawn out disputes over the house and child support. But the agreement was that we would communicate through our attorneys. Why was he calling me now?

"What do you want?" I asked with icicles in my voice.

"I know you're angry, but please listen to what I have to say. I'm in jail."

"And?"

"I've made a very big mistake, Isabel. I should have never stayed with this woman. Right now, I can honestly say I hate her. She's a witch, and I think she put a spell on me so I couldn't see the truth. She's made my life miserable!" he said, starting to sob.

"How sad," I said, my voice suffused with sarcasm. "So why are you in jail? Did you kill her?"

"Please don't joke. This is very serious. Just let me finish."

I vacillated between hanging up or listening to this unfolding melodrama. "Go on," I finally said.

"She's driving me crazy with her jealousy, and she's too controlling. Get this. The other day, I wanted to call the kids, and she took the phone and hit me on the head with it and made a big gash on my forehead. She's a thief who likes to shoplift..."

"Get to the jail part. I'm at work, and I don't have all day."

"Okay. Yesterday we had a big fight, and I told her to leave. She got pissed off and started to hit me. Then she started to break my things, and when she smashed my computer, I lost it. I punched her and dragged her by her hair to the door and kicked her out. The next thing I knew, she was at my door with the police. She pressed charges against me and even told them I had drugs in the apartment. That's how I got arrested. Isabel...I want to come home."

He was crying uncontrollably, and I didn't have it in me to belittle him or come back with "I told you so." The longer he cried, the sorrier I felt for him. The ball was again in my court.

"Eron, I don't know...How can I trust you again?"

"Please let me come back, and I'll prove myself to you," he said, barely able to get the words out. "I'm through with this woman. I never want to see her again. Give me time to show you that I can be the man I should have been. I am truly sorry that I put you and the kids through this, but it's over. Please let me come home."

"Eron I don't know if I can trust you anymore. I'm so worried that you will change your mind again."

"Isabel, I promise you, it will never happen again."

Two days later, Eron was back in Florida.

He looked like a changed man, with an air of exuberance I hadn't seen since the day he proposed. The children were thrilled to see him. It was a new beginning, a chance to do it over and get it right.

That evening, he took me out to dinner and then dancing. It was like being out on a date with the man I had first met. During the meal, we made plans to return to New York, and the very next day, I booked flights for a departure two days away.

The day before our flight, I took the kids out of school, canceled the utilities, arranged with a realtor to sell the house, and submitted my resignation to Cindy. The kids and I excitedly packed our belongings and got rid of stuff we wouldn't need. We were set to go.

We were going to put this all behind us and be a family again. This had been a harsh lesson for both of us, but maybe it was the wake-up call we needed to make our union stronger.

The morning of our departure, I went to the supermarket and got a few breakfast items and snacks for the kids. When I returned to the house, Eron was just getting off the phone.

"Who was that?" I asked.

"I just called Marla to let her know that I'm coming back with my family and that she needs to be out of my apartment before we get there."

"Oh. I didn't realize she was still in the apartment."

"Well, she won't be by the time we get there. I've run out of cigarettes, so I'm going to the store, and I'll be right back," he said.

"Okay, but don't take too long. You won't want to eat cold eggs."

I quickly made breakfast and sat the kids down to eat. It was taking Eron an awfully long time to return, and I began to get worried. As the taxi would be arriving soon to take us to the airport, I put our bags by the door, made sure the kids were ready, and gave the house a final run-through.

I was standing in the kitchen when Eron walked through the door.

Something was not right. Eron looked like he had been crying.

"What's wrong?" I asked.

He just stood there looking at me with glistening eyes, and his silence was sickeningly clear.

"No...no. Please don't tell me. You've changed your mind, Eron? You've changed your mind?" I screamed.

He started to cry.

"How can you do this to us, Eron? How can you do this!" I was hysterical. "Help me understand. For God's sake, please make sense of this!"

The children were still standing by the door, staring at us.

He pulled me into the bedroom and sat on our bed.

"Isabel, this is very hard for me to say, but I don't want to do this anymore. I tried, but it's not going to work. I want to be honest with you and my intent is not to hurt you. The truth is that you have changed so much. You look better now, but I'm just not physically attracted to you. Marla...well... she's very sexy, and she makes me feel like a man again. Isabel, I'm still young, and I need to feel the kind of sexual attraction a man feels for a woman, and with you..."

I raised my hand and slapped him hard. "Get out! The taxi's waiting for you, you son-of-a-bitch! Get out now!"

He quietly got up, picked up his suitcase, and walked out of our lives forever.

19

Picking Up the Pieces

Our divorce was finalized after a lengthy dispute over Eron's demands through his attorney. He wanted me to sell the house after the kids turned eighteen and give him half of the net proceeds, and he refused to pay for their health insurance. I was having none of it. I finally settled for keeping the house indefinitely, no health insurance, and a pittance for child support against my lawyer's better judgment. It was the best I could do to get this nightmare over with.

Months later, I called Eron at work and left a message that the children and I would be visiting New York and did he want to see them. Evidently, Eron was jotting down my phone numbers from caller ID and leaving them where his woman could find them.

I received a voicemail from her: "If you bother my husband at work again, I will get you fired from your job and you will never see him again. He does what I say. Okay, honey? And don't you forget it."

It didn't stop there. She embarked on a malicious campaign of harassment with silent phone calls to my home and job. Countless subscriptions to weight management magazines were mailed to me with her name on them.

A year later, I got a subscription to *Parents Magazine* labeled with both their names. At 2:30 a.m. my phone rang, and I let my answering machine pick up the call. A short period of silence was followed by the cry of a newborn.

I decided to write her a short note:

I am happier now than I've ever been. Your calls are pointless and immature, but if that's your only way of putting some fun into your pathetic life, then knock yourself out. I'm glad you're together. You deserve each other.

The calls stopped.

Slowly I began to put our lives back in order and move on without Eron, but it wasn't easy. I read books, met with counselors, and talked to women who'd been there, needlessly trying to find the answers to his motivations and actions. Instead, I should have been challenging myself to unravel my twisted obsession and disentangle that once-spirited soul that had gotten lost in this relationship.

I went into a deep depression and tried to pacify myself by spending money I didn't have. Buying all the things the kids and I could never have and doing the things we could never do while I was married to Eron gave me a vindictive pleasure. I literally picked up my life from where I had left off just before I met him.

Although I was forty years old, I reverted to my dance hall days and gathered a colorful and fun-loving entourage. I lived my life through them, blending into their lifestyles like a chameleon. Alone, I'd wallow in self-pity and cry for the lonely child inside me, the little girl who borrowed dreams and embellished them like the revamped hand-me-down clothes she once wore.

"Hey Julita, what're you doing tonight?"

"Isabel, I'm glad you called. My friend and I are going to this new Latin club that opened up downtown. Wanna go?"

"Sure! How about I invite Millie and Raquel? They're always up for a good time."

"Why not? I'll pick you girls up around 9:30. Can you be ready by then?"

"I'll be ready!" I said.

Within forty-five minutes, I had showered and put on my Madonna bustier and spike-heeled shoes, ready for a rowdy ladies' night out.

My living room soon became a bustling coop of cackling hens, all dressed to the nines. My co-worker Millie arrived first. The epitome of Latina sultriness, her hourglass figure turned many heads, both male and female. Her perfectly manicured red nails flashed as she flit her slender hands in exaggerated movements when she spoke. Millie was the sexiest grandmother I had ever met who played the field like a wanton vamp. Two drinks and anything went.

"Girl, you look fantastic," she said as she warmly hugged me.

"So do you!" I replied, taking her hand and giving her a spin.

The doorbell rang and in sashayed Raquel. Model-thin and statuesque with tawny skin and sparkling hazel eyes, her long chestnut hair flowed onto her bare shoulders like rippled rivulets on a sandy shore. The mother of three teenaged boys, it baffled me how she managed to stay so thin and beautiful.

"So Raquel, have you decided to stay in Florida for good? I asked her.

"I love it here, my boys like it here, and if my husband doesn't want to live in Florida, he can stay in New York for all I care."

"Wow," slurred Millie in her nasal voice, "are you planning to break up with him? I mean, how is this going to work if he's there and you're here?"

"It's not. I've asked him for a divorce, and he doesn't want one. I don't know what he's thinking, but I'm done. I'm not in love with him anymore. I've told him so many times, and he doesn't get it."

"Jeez, you told him just like that?" I asked.

"It pisses me off when I have to repeat myself. I have to be strong with him, or I'll be stuck like this forever. *Basta ya, chica*! Enough is enough."

At that moment, the doorbell rang again. It was Julita and her friend.

"Hey girls! *Ave Maria, que olores*! What's with all the perfume? It smells here like Chichi's bordello," Julita remarked. Turning to her companion, "They don't always smell this way." Her speechless friend smiled timidly.

"Girls, meet Zoraida. Zoraida meet Isabel la Madonna, Millie la Madama, y Raquel la modelo." Everyone broke out in riotous laughter.

I could tell that Zoraida wasn't exactly like the rest of us middle-aged debutantes. Her unblemished café latte visage had little makeup except for a dab of lipstick and a hint of blush. Her thin, chin-length brown hair was combed simply in place. A glittery blouse over dark slacks and low-heeled pumps were her basic ensemble. But the light and warmth from her neon smile was overwhelming.

"Let's go," I said. "I want to get there early so we can grab a ringside table by the bar. Best place to view the line-up, you know."

Julita's car wobbled as five latinalicious free spirits stuffed their expanding derrieres into her compact caravan.

"So what's your story, Zoraida?" I asked her once we were settled in.

"Well, I'm divorced, I have two teen-aged boys, and I'm a teacher at Parkway Middle School. I love my salsa music, love to dance, and I paint as a hobby. Oh, and I'm back in school doing my PhD. That's pretty much it in a nutshell." Her last sentence was punctuated with that toothy, blinding smile.

"Wow, you sound busy! Hey, my buddy Evelyn works there too. Do you know her?" I asked.

"The name sounds familiar, but I can't put a face to it."

"We'll have to go out for lunch sometime, and I'll introduce you. Evelyn doesn't go out dancing much but she's always down for food and a good laugh."

We took turns telling Zoraida a little about ourselves and how we all ended up as single women stuffed like sardines in Julita's car on our way to a Latin club.

Whenever we got together for a ladies' night out, our aim was not to pick up men, though subconsciously we craved the attention. For women who had crawled out of ego-stripping relationships, we simply yearned for validation that, yes woman, you're still attractive enough to catch my eye. None of us ever took anyone home. Well...maybe Millie.

More importantly, we enjoyed each other's company. We were free to be ourselves and to laugh. Even the most hurtful situation could be turned into a one-woman comedic skit with a captive, empathetic audience.

At the club, we took a table by the bar, where a couple of men had already assumed the stud pose. "Oye Raquel, that guy at the bar with the black shirt and medallion stuck on his chest hair keeps staring at you," I said.

"Ay, no, he looks young enough to be my son."

"How would he know that unless you tell him? Go on, girl. Make his night."

Zoraida tapped me on the shoulder. It's the only way to get someone's attention in a loud Latin club. "Isabel, I think that man wants to dance with you."

Standing a few feet away was an older version of Cantinflas the clown, wearing a polyester striped jacket and making a circle sign with a down-turned index finger. I politely declined by shouting to him that I was tired. We do have our limits.

Raquel was now on the dance floor, getting down to a hot mambo with Kid Medallion, and Julita was being twirled like a top by a drop-dead-gorgeous Dominicano. Later she told us that he'd asked for her number, and she had given him the wrong one.

"Why did you do that?" I asked her.

"He smelled married," she said. Yet another survival skill we acquire through experience.

That night we danced until the place closed.

"Where's Millie?" I asked looking around. I finally caught sight of her at the bar. She had a young bartender up against the wall and was pulling his tie off.

"Millie, leave that boy alone. Can't you see he's afraid of you?" I said trying to pull her away.

"No, wait," she slurred. Turning to the coy kitten, "What's your name? How old are you? You got a girlfriend?"

"Millie, let's go!" I grabbed her by her claw and dragged her from her petrified prey.

We went out to an all-night eatery afterwards and laughed until the sun came up.

The following weekend, my new friend Zoraida and I made plans to go clubbing at another Latin nightspot.

"I want you to meet my friend, Mickey," she said. "He's a good dancer, and if we don't get asked to dance, he can be our partner."

"Sounds like a plan," I said.

Mickey appeared to be in his late thirties. Of medium build and stature with short curly hair, dark bulbous eyes, and a somewhat protuberant nose, he was dressed very smartly in a designer shirt and perfectly pressed slacks. He was not a looker, but his outrageous personality more than made up for any physical imperfections. His thick Spanish accent was interlaced with a pronounced effeminate lilt. My gaydar wires went ballistic.

Mickey and I became almost inseparable. When we weren't physically together, we were on the phone yakking and laughing. He injected humor into everything he said and did. It wasn't that he looked at the world through rose-colored glasses. On the contrary, he was levelheaded and realistic about life, except for one issue.

Mickey was almost forty now and still lived with his parents. I wasn't sure if he had ever come to terms with his homosexuality, nor did I ask. I figured if he ever wanted me to know, he would tell me.

"Hello woman, you're not going to believe where I was this past week," said Mickey in one of our frequent phone conversations.

"Let me guess. You went alligator hunting in the Everglades."

"Wrong. I'm scared of things that snap, and where would I sleep?"

"Okay, I give up. Where were you?"

"I went to the Grand Canyon! Isabel, I have always wanted to see it, and it was fabulous! I went with some friends, and we went on a helicopter ride over the canyons. Picture this: red sunset over the horizon, copper mountains with deep valleys and nothing moving but the occasional ant crawling up a mountain."

"Get out!"

"Okay, maybe it was a hiker, but that's what it looked like from my angle."

"How could you stand being so high up looking down into the valleys? I would have fainted," I said.

"Oh it wasn't pretty. At first I was screaming like Fay Wray in King Kong's paw, but you get used to it."

I laughed until my cheeks hurt. "Okay, Mickey, time out. I was almost incontinent there."

"Speaking of incontinent, how's your old friend Yolanda? Is she still moping and moaning?"

"Honestly, I don't get to speak to her that often."

"I don't blame you, woman. You know, I'm a simple and sensible man. I don't take too many things to heart, and when I do, I keep them to myself. Now Yolanda, that woman needs to get a life. Her conversations are so boring and everything bothers her. What makes her think people want to hear her ca-ca? If I was her, I'd shoot myself."

"Mickey, don't say that. She just doesn't have the gift of gab that you have."

"Listen woman, if life is not worth living, it's not worth talking about. Please feel free to deprive me of your doom and gloom."

"True, but I wouldn't go so far as to do myself in because my life was a still-life painting. What if I discovered at the pearly gates that tomorrow I would have won the lotto or run into my prince charming? Wouldn't I feel like an idiot then?" I said.

"Oh yes, spoken like a true optimist. I'm an optimist too, at least until they start moving animals in pairs to the Kennedy Space Center."

We gabbed for another hour before we finally ran out of things to say. Well, I did. "I leave you with priceless words of wisdom from the great Confucius," Mickey said. "Man who walk thru airport turnstile sideways going to Bangkok."

"Shut up!" I was still laughing long after I hung up the phone.

We went out to a local bar with a few of Mickey's co-workers, and he got seriously drunk. He stumbled out of the bar behind me, and when I looked back, he was just standing there, frozen. "What's wrong Mickey?"

"Woman, I think I'm gay, a fag, un homosexual." His facial expression was one of shock, as if this was a novel revelation.

"Mickey, I know and it's okay. There's nothing wrong with that."

"No, you don't understand," he said, and he went on to tell me about being molested as a young boy by a family friend and how humiliated he had felt. I listened to him while he revealed this dark secret in choppy thoughts, like a child relating a frightening event.

"Mickey, I'm so sorry this happened to you. You didn't ask for it, and you surely didn't deserve it. But what happened to you has nothing to do with you being gay. You just are, and it's okay. Some people may not understand it or accept it, but don't be afraid to be yourself when you're with me."

He never brought the subject up again.

I finally got Zoraida and Evelyn to meet, and whenever we got a chance, we'd go out for dinner and talk and tell stories for hours over frozen margaritas. Evelyn had fallen for a guy who kept whining about her weight but wouldn't leave her. Zoraida shared news on the latest sociopolitical issues affecting the world. I had my usual banal stories. It all made for interesting conversation.

Eventually, I lost touch with Julita after she broke her ankle and couldn't get around like she used to.

I had also lost contact with Raquel, the beautiful mocha temptress with olive eyes, until I saw her one day at the drug store. Her eyes were sunken and glassy, her skin weatherbeaten, her face lean and tired.

She introduced the scruffy cowboy she was with as her boyfriend. I did my best to hide the shock and sadness I felt seeing her this way. I wondered where her boys were and if she felt happier with the drifter she was with than with her husband, but I didn't ask. She excitedly told me that she and her boyfriend were moving to north Florida, and she almost convinced me that she was truly content.

Months later, my neighbor, who had introduced me to Raquel, came knocking at my door. She sat at my kitchen table with a glum look on her face.

"Isabel, I know Raquel was a good friend of yours, and it saddens me to have to tell you this. Raquel was killed. We don't know all the details, but apparently that coward she was with beat her to death."

Even sadder than her untimely death was watching Raquel's boys, now young men, crying inconsolably at her funeral. She had made an unfortunate choice, and its consequences were devastating beyond anything she could have ever imagined.

I continued to spend money until my credit card debts got so high, that twice I refinanced the house to bring them under control. As if that wasn't a harsh enough predicament, Eron stopped paying child support for over a year, burying me in an even deeper hole. Within two years, my reckless spending had spiraled out of control, and I filed for bankruptcy. I lost all of the possessions I had impulsively bought, selling all of my furnishings piece by piece just to pay for our basic necessities.

I found myself counting pennies to buy food and asking friends and co-workers for a few dollars to make it through the week. There were days when I'd call in sick to work because I didn't have enough gas to get me to the office and back. I knocked on my church's door on several occasions and at the local community pantry for food. I became one of the people who stood on WIC lines for government-issued provisions and sent beg letters to radio stations for Christmas gifts for my children.

Mickey had lost his job, but bless his heart, he gave me groceries whenever he could and loaned me money from his credit card to pay essential bills. Zoraida and Evelyn stuck by me, and though they couldn't help me financially, they gave me their support and steadfast friendship.

My sister Bernie and brother Gil sent whatever they could afford from time to time, but through all of this, I received no phone calls, no words of support from Mother. I asked her once outright why she never called me, and she simply said, "Because I can't stand to hear you cry."

So many helped in little ways, but asking for handouts was humiliating and demoralizing. The bottom line came one day when I took my children to the grand opening of a supermarket so that they could eat from the snacks they were offering.

"Zoraida, Evelyn, I'm at the end of my rope, and I feel like I have to do something to change my life," I told my friends as they sat at my kitchen table one day. "I can't continue to live like this and put my children through the suffering that I've brought on them."

"What do you want to do? What can you do?" asked Evelyn.

"I've come up with a plan that may be risky and will take a lot out of me, but if I make it, I'll be set for life."

"Okay, shoot. Let's hear it," said Zoraida.

"It's nothing illegal, is it?" asked Evelyn.

"Ave Maria, Evelyn, let her talk," said Zoraida.

"You girls know that my dream has always been to work in the medical field. I found out last week that there's a nursing program starting at a technical school, and it's just down the road from here. The problem is that it's offered during the day, and obviously I have to work to pay my bills."

Evelyn and Zoraida listened intently as they punctuated each of my sentences with, "Yeah?"

"I decided to take a night job so that I can go to school during the day. There's an opening on the nursing unit for a technician on nights to watch their patients on heart monitors and interpret their rhythms. But for me to take this job, I would need to take a pay cut."

"Can you afford to do that?" asked Evelyn.

"I don't have a choice. I see no other way out. The other problem is that they're requiring that I take an EKG course way up in Orlando, and I can't drive there. You know, my panic attacks. But I found out that there's a bus that goes there..."

"No problem. I'll drive you there," said Zoraida.

"No Zori, it's a six-week program, and if you take me, you would have to bring me back home, and I can't do that to you."

"I said I'll take you. Problem solved. I don't want to hear it. Next issue," said Zoraida.

I passed the EKG course, got the night job, and started school.

It was an insanely intense year of struggling to make ends meet, straining to stay awake after days of sleep deprivation, and fighting just to keep my head above water.

My nursing instructors, although aware of my situation, were pitiless. I was publicly embarrassed when I'd start to fall asleep in class and humiliated in front of everyone whenever I got to class late. I was expected to perform like everyone else, no excuses. I fought to maintain their standards for failure was not an option, though there were times towards the end when I thought I would lose my mind.

"Mickey, my sanity is hanging by a thin thread. I don't know how long I can keep this up."

"Now you listen, woman. You know that I'm a sensible man, right? If I thought you couldn't do this, I would tell you. But you can and you will. Just take it one day at a time. Besides, I've already picked out the outfit I'm wearing to your graduation party."

"You might be wearing it to my funeral if this gets any harder."

By now, Aimée was fourteen years old and Daniel was eight. Aimée took over the housework and cooking and care of her brother, who silently went along without ever complaining or questioning why things were so hard and why we had to do without.

On weekdays, when I'd rush home from school to take a two-hour nap before starting my twelve-hour shift, Aimée would be sitting at the table helping her brother with homework while preparing a meal and a bagged dinner for me to take to work.

After several months, we began clinical practice, which required that students meet at a hospital at 6:00 a.m. I'd wake the kids up at 5:00 a.m., drive them to my nursing director's church and leave them at the front in pitch black darkness until the doors opened at 6:30 a.m. From there, the director would pick them up and drive them to school. I'd hug them good bye, jump in my car, and cry all the way to the hospital.

It was because of my children that I found the fortitude to keep pushing forward.

Three months into the program, my house went into foreclosure. The spiritualist had been right. That house was never a home but the entombment of false illusions and broken dreams. I was secretly glad to be rid of it.

The struggle of trying to hold on to it was draining me, and I needed to stay focused.

As we were driving home from Aimée's school one day, we came upon a brand new apartment complex with a British theme. A large banner across the front read, "Di and Charles welcome you to your new home – Wellington Apartments." It called out to me like an enchanting book of childhood fantasies on a library shelf beckoning to be read.

They did a credit check while I waited with a lump in my throat, but thankfully the foreclosure didn't appear.

A week later, we moved into a beautiful three-bedroom apartment. I had packed everything I could fit into a small rental van, except for one item. As I prepared to leave, I wondered what the new homeowners would think when they discovered a simple white wedding gown hanging in a dark corner of the master bedroom's closet.

While shutting the front door, I caught a strong whiff of incense and cigar smoke. Smiling to myself, I walked away and never looked back.

I graduated from nursing school on a brilliant, sun-drenched day in May, 1995. My children and my good friends Zoraida, Mickey, and Cindy my former supervisor, were there, as well as several co-workers who knew of my grueling climb to that climatic moment. It was then, when the weight of our struggle was finally lifted, that I came to terms with what I had accomplished against all odds.

I walked onstage with wobbly knees, accepted my diploma, and gave a short speech. "I want to thank my friends who stood by me and supported me when I couldn't stand on my own; my co-workers who helped and inspired me. But mostly, I want to thank my children, Aimée and Daniel." I paused on the verge of breaking down. "I hope that you are as proud of me today as I am of you."

A loud cheer went up in the auditorium as my friends and co-workers stood and clapped. I felt such a euphoric rush of relief and pride. I looked at my children and shouted with fists in air, "I did it! We made it! We did it!" It was my one moment in time.

Life changed dramatically. I passed my licensing exam on my first attempt and was hired shortly after as a nurse on the medical-surgical unit of the hospital. It took several months to rectify the financial disaster I had created, but in the end, I had redeemed myself, and I was finally, definitively free.

"Isabel, there's something wrong with, me" said Mickey, his voice shaking.

"What's wrong Mickey? What's happening?"

"It's kind of embarrassing, but I've been bleeding and I'm losing a lot of weight."

"Go to the emergency room right now and call me back."

Mickey did as I suggested and was admitted to a local hospital where he received an immediate blood transfusion. Using my medical knowledge, I tried to make sense of what was happening to him. Every time I went to see him, he'd say that they were still running tests and weren't sure.

Three weeks later, he was still hospitalized. I was watching Mickey deteriorate, and I had nothing to prepare me for an outcome, good or bad. I stopped asking questions as it became clear that he didn't want me to know. The dreaded condition became clear to me, but Mickey was strong, and he would fight for life.

I had to work several shifts over a long weekend and finally got home, ready to collapse on my bed and sleep off the fatigue.

Just as I was dozing off, the phone rang. It was Zoraida. "You need to come to the hospital quick. Mickey took a turn for the worse, and he's in intensive care. You need to prepare yourself. He looks bad."

I got dressed and rushed to the hospital, hoping that it wasn't as bad as Zoraida had insinuated.

I hugged Mickey's father, who was sitting in a waiting room, and asked him about Mickey.

"I'm not ready for this. I never thought something like this could happen to him," he said sobbing. "*Mi hijo querido*, my beloved son. I wish he had told me. I would love him just the same. He is a good son. I don't understand why this happen to him."

"Papá, I have no answers for you. I don't understand it myself, how something like this could happen to someone like Mickey. Your son is very special to many people, and maybe all our prayers will bring him back to health."

"No, no I don't think this will happen. Go see him. He is not good."

I left his father and went up to the intensive care unit. Zoraida was pacing outside an isolation cubicle.

"Where is he?" I asked her.

"In there," she said, pointing to the glass encased room.

This could not possibly be Mickey! My beautiful friend, the one who passionately embraced life and had brought so much joy to mine, was almost unrecognizable. He was ghostly pale with ventilator and nasogastric tubes taped to his face. Blood was dripping from his mouth. I called his name, and he opened his eyes and fought to speak.

"It's okay, Mickey. There's no need to speak. I know what you're thinking. Try to stay calm, and don't be afraid. You're in good hands and you're going to be okay. Just close your eyes and try to relax. I'll stay here until you fall asleep." He stopped fighting and gently closed his eyes.

Outside the ICU, I fell apart in Zoraida's arms. "I wish I had never come," I cried. "This is not the way I want to remember him. I can't believe this is happening, Zori!"

"This was your chance to say good-bye. How you remember him is up to you," she said.

Somehow I made it home through a haze of tears. Sitting in the darkness of my bedroom, I lit a candle, closed my eyes, and tried to connect with Mickey's fading spirit. I visualized him flying high above the Grand Canyon, soaring like a superhero, making curlicue and spiral ribbons in the sky; laughing and screaming like a child on a roller coaster ride, rising steeply and falling on a rainbow's undulating tracks. "Look at me, Isabel! I can fly!"

I watched him gently land at the mouth of a dark tunnel. He looked confused, then disappointed. He put his hands in his front jeans pockets, like he always did, shrugged his shoulders and said, "I guess the ride's over. Oh well, it was fun while it lasted."

A light appeared at the deep end of the tunnel. He looked behind him, then at me, hesitant to move.

"It's okay, Mickey. Don't be afraid. You have friends and loved ones waiting for you. Just promise you won't forget me."

"I won't forget you, woman." He timidly waved good-bye and walked into the light.

Seconds later, I opened my eyes. The candle on my night-stand had blown out.

My phone rang.

"Isabel..."

"I know, Zori," I said.

Mickey was cremated and his ashes strewn over the aqua blue waters near his hometown in Puerto Rico. I didn't go to the prayer service at his parents' house. I couldn't stand the thought of entering their apartment and not seeing him there.

To this day, I can feel his spirit around me, uplifting me in times of need, celebrating with me in times of joy. I talk to him often in my meditative moments, and I can hear him respond in his indelible way, "Woman, you know I'm a simple and sensible man..."

Life went on without my Mickey, but it wasn't the same. Zoraida and Evelyn, my pillars of comfort, were never more than a phone call away. But life had lost its luster. The party was over.

I wholly immersed myself in the challenges of motherhood. My children were quickly maturing and developing their distinct personalities in unsubtle ways, and I needed to be there for them.

Daniel had grown into a reticent, reclusive ten-year-old whose prodded efforts to socialize were met with taunts from bullies. Numerous meetings at school made no improvement. He remained quiet and shy, preferring to play in his room with his imaginary friends. In time, my son's shyness turned into a crippling social phobia.

"Mom, Daniel wouldn't get on the school bus this morning," Aimée said one day.

"Why not, Daniel?" I asked him.

"Nobody lets me sit next to them. And they call me names."

"Have you told this to the bus driver?"

Aimée cut in, "He won't talk. He won't speak up for himself. The bus drivers don't care. They won't do anything."

"So what do you do, Daniel? Where do you sit?"

"Sometimes in the back if there's space. Sometimes I just stand all the way to school."

"Oh no, this won't do. I'll have a word with the principal tomorrow. Is that all right with you, Daniel?"

"I guess," he said.

"How about I treat you guys to dinner?" I asked, trying to bring some enthusiasm into the dismal mood.

"Great!" Aimée said.

"Can I stay home, Momma?" Daniel asked. "I don't mind making myself macaroni and cheese."

"Oh, Daniel," I said. "I would really like it if you'd come with us. I know it's uncomfortable for you, but the only way to get over your shyness is to confront your fears. Aimée and I will be with you, and you can have anything you like."

"C'mon Daniel," Aimée coaxed. "You can have a nice burger instead of macaroni and cheese."

He mulled it over for a few seconds. "Okay, I'll go."

At the restaurant, the waitress took our orders. "And what will you have, young man?"

He remained silent, not making eye contact with the waitress. He looked at me, his eyes pleading for me to rescue him. It was not my intent to torture my son, but it was clear that he needed the kind of help I could no longer provide.

"He'll have a cheeseburger and a coke," I said.

At sixteen, Aimée was completely the opposite. Fiercely independent and worldly, she had no qualms about speaking her mind.

"Momma, when are we going to do something fun together? I'm so sick of being stuck in this apartment with nothing to do. I don't even have any friends to hang out with. School is boring as hell! I feel so depressed, like my life is going nowhere!" Aimée cried.

"Pumpernickel, where did all of this come from? You're too young to be thinking like that."

"Well, that's how I feel."

"Aimée, times have changed for us, and they're bound to get even better. I know they will," I said with conviction.

"But when? You keep saying that, but nothing ever changes. You're waiting for miracles that are never going to happen!"

"Aimée, if you can't believe in miracles, then believe in yourself. When you want something bad enough, let that drive push you to make it happen. Sometimes you'll run into brick walls that are put there to test you. Find a way around them and stay focused on your dream. Where there's a will, there's a way. Always remember that."

"It's not that easy, Mom."

"No, it's not easy. Some of us have to work very hard for what we want. What is it that you want? What would you like to do more than anything?" I asked her.

"I want to do something different and fun. When I get older, I want to see the world, like you did Momma when you were young."

An outrageous idea popped into my head. Could I possibly pull this off? "I'm going to prove to you that if you want something bad enough, there's always a way, no matter how difficult it may seem."

Her eyes suddenly lit up. "What are you going to do?"

"You'll see," I said.

It took me months of pinching pennies and doing without, much to Aimée's frustration, for things had to get worse before they got better. That's what I kept telling her whenever she became disheartened.

I told the girls at work that I was planning a big surprise for my kids, and if I could make it happen, it would be nothing short of a miracle. I didn't give them any details just in case it didn't work out.

One evening, I pulled out my old album with pictures of my trip to Paris and London. I told Aimée and Daniel the detailed story of how a girl from El Barrio had managed to achieve the unimaginable. "This is my favorite picture," I said, pointing to the one taken in front of the Eiffel Tower.

"Wow, Momma, that is awesome!" Aimée said.

"Yeah, that's pretty cool!" Daniel remarked.

"I would love to see it. Maybe someday we could go," Aimée said as she turned the page.

There was the envelope I had placed with her and Daniel's name.

"What's this, Momma?" Aimée asked.

"It's tickets for all of us to go to London and Paris."

"Are you serious?"

"Yes, I am serious! We leave the day after tomorrow."

"Wow," Daniel said. "Do they have McDonald's there?"

"Oh, Daniel!" I said, tousling his hair.

We stayed for twenty-one days and did it all on a back-packer's budget. We toured all the famous landmarks in London, traveled on the underground and on double-decker buses, and visited all the free museums. We were there for the Queen's birthday celebration and witnessed the changing of the guard. To Daniel's great delight, McDonald's was everywhere.

Midway through our stay, we took a ferry across the English Channel to France. In Paris, we climbed the lofty steps to the Sacré Coeur Church, picnicked on the lawn of Notre Dame, and walked down the Champs Elysée to the Arc de Triomphe. At the Eiffel Tower, Aimée took a picture of me on the very spot where I had stood twenty-five years before. That unforgettable moment brought tears to my eyes.

In years to come, this experience would prove to be life-changing for all of us. I sent a picture postcard from Paris to my co-workers, and on the back I simply wrote, "I did it!"

20

Las Chancletas (The Slippers)

It was time for Las Chancletas' semi-annual bare-your-dirty-linen gossip fest. That's what we decided to call our intimate circle of friendship, for we were as loyal and steadfast as an old pair of slippers. Life events and personal responsibilities may have taken up much of our time in the ten years we had known each other, but our scheduled get-togethers were sacrosanct and unbreakable, as was our bond.

Nothing is more fun than three Latinas yakking about their lives and woes, English mixed with Spanish, punctuated with riotous laughter over endless hours, much to the chagrin of our poor server.

"*Bueno, mi'ja,* what have you been up to?" Zori asked Evelyn.

Evelyn pushed her left hand towards us to reveal a gorgeous ring with exquisite sparkling rocks. She has an uncanny ability to date men who shower her with expensive gifts in spite of her rotundity, a source of grievance and self-reproach. Nevertheless, my go-braless, thong-wearing friend will most certainly tell all about her latest beau with titillating, mouth-dropping details.

"Where did you get that?" asked Zoraida in shock.

"Explain this now. I think I'm going to throw up," I said. "Don't tell me this is from the Colombiano who thinks you're too heavy."

"Nope," she said with a wicked smile. "He's out of the picture. This is from a very sweet older guy I met who's fallen madly in love with me. And it's just a friendship ring, nothing more. What do you think?"

"It's decadent. What do you mean older?" asked Zori.

"Yeah, what do you mean older?" I echoed. "You got a picture of him?"

"As a matter of fact, I do. And please don't rag on his looks. He's a very nice man." She handed his picture to Zori.

"Ooookaaay..." Zori said and handed the picture to me.

"Jeez, Evelyn, don't you think he's a little too old for you?" I asked as Zori grabbed the photo for another look.

"Well, you can't really see it 'cause it's white, but he's got a little band of hair along the back and sides of his head. I think the angle of the camera makes him look older."

"Do you guys have anything in common? Can he still have sex?" asked Zoraida.

"Yes, he can," she said defensively as she snatched the picture back from Zori.

"Well, okay. As long as he's sincere and makes you happy, that's all that counts, "I said.

"No, now let's be realistic here," said Zori the sage. "No money, no honey. I don't care if he's got his own teeth and a head full of hair. If a man ain't got his own money, he's not coming home with me. I already raised two kids. I'm not supporting a grown man."

A server appeared with a platter full of chicken wings and we all dug in. "So is that your only criteria?" I asked Zori. "Because Iris Chacón over here knows where to find them."

"No, that's not true," said Evelyn. "They find me. I don't purposely look for men with money, but if they want to shower me with gifts, why should I refuse?"

"I wouldn't refuse either," said Zori. "My criteria are simple, Isabel: physical chemistry, intelligence, a good sense of humor, and his own bank account, and not necessarily in that order. Realistically, the chances of finding such a beast at my age are slim to none. I'm prepared to live my life alone because, honestly, I'm too old for games, baggage, and annoying habits."

"What about you, Isabel?" Evelyn asked.

"I'm not looking for anyone, but every now and then, I think it might be nice to share my life with someone who's a good conversationalist and with whom I can have a good laugh. Sex and money are good, but to have a unique friendship with someone would be awesome."

"What are you saying, woman? No sex?" asked Evelyn.

"Sex is not high on my list. I just want someone to like me for who I am; someone with the gift of laughter, intelligent, worldly and spontaneous. And those are hard things to come by in one package, especially when you're as nutty and unpredictable as I am."

"You definitely got a point there, Miss Bette," said Zori. "On that note, let's have a toast. To las chancletas: here's to us girls with the high-heeled shoes; we spend their money and drink their booze. We may have no cherry, but that's no sin. We still have the box that it came in!"

"Wepa!"

"Salud!"

21

Epilogue

I love my job. Some days I repeated those words to convince myself, and some days I really meant them. I worked as a medical-surgical nurse for twenty-eight years, and though it took some time to get used to the stress, the rewards far outweighed the unpleasant moments.

I cared for people from all walks of life with an assortment of ailments, accidents, and anomalies. Like Forrest's box of chocolates, I never knew what I was going to get, which made my work that much more interesting.

Over the years, I remembered mostly the ones that in dying, taught me how to live. Some I befriended and followed their steps towards recovery or final release. In many ways, I felt that I had redeemed myself in Grandma's eyes, for it was her legacy that I carried with me and imparted to those I looked after. I was where I needed to be.

During that time, my love of reading turned into a passion for writing.

"I've kept all the letters you've ever written to me, and if you don't write something soon, I'm sending them to Oprah," said my good friend Evelyn one day.

So with the threat of Oprah reading my unedited letters and pithy comments, I began to painstakingly pen my story.

In 2010, I submitted an excerpt of my memoir, still in manuscript form, to Authonomy, a HarperCollins writers' group where authors exchanged feedback on each other's work while hoping to catch the eye of the renowned publisher—yet another move that turned out to be serendipitous.

There were many talented authors there, but one in particular caught my eye. His name was Barry Harden, and he'd written a brilliant memoir of growing up literally on his own and navigating the tough streets of London from an astonishingly early age. His life story, written in an unapologetic literary style, touched me deeply.

He was a writer who seemed to have stepped straight from the pages of my favorite storyteller, Dickens. Barry carried the weight of deprivation, loneliness, and quiet humility like a familiar, frayed coat.

I fell in love with the way he saw the world—with the tenderness beneath his scars. And like the forgotten boys of Dickens' London, he had never been given much, but he possessed a mind rich with stories and a heart still capable of love.

He was moved by my review and incredulous that someone thought his writing was that good. We communicated for a brief time, neither knowing of our then marital status or personal challenges.

A few years later, out of the blue, I received a message from him on LinkedIn. "Are you the Isabel from Authonomy?" Later, he'd write, "You know, I never forgot you."

He had been living in France at the time in a decades-long marriage that sadly perpetuated the emotional abuse he experienced in his youth.

I was in a twenty-two year platonic partnership under similar circumstances, which deserves no more mention than these few lines, except to say that, this time, I made the choice to move on. The stress and hardship of undoing all that we had built was no longer an excuse to stay on at the expense of my self-respect.

Barry and I continued to write daily, his humility and kindness drawing me closer with every conversation. He spoke as though the world was a story still unfolding, and with him, I wanted to write every chapter.

Together, we have built a life I have never known—a life filled with laughter, late-night musings, and a sense of belonging that feels real and effortless. In his presence, I found not only love but a partner who saw the world—and me—with a profound and beautiful clarity.

I gathered his overlooked manuscripts, meticulously re-fining each page before sending them off to publishers. Now, three of his works, including his memoir, have found their way into the world.

A few years ago, my daughter Aimée sent me a postcard from England. "Mom, you're not going to believe where

I'm standing—Penny Lane in Liverpool." In my youth, I had fantasized about being where my daughter stood. When our dreams don't come true, sometimes we can hand them down to our children and hope that they will come true for them. The joy can be immeasurable just the same.

Later she wrote from London, where she had been doing her master's degree, "Even though the day has been rough, there is always another horizon. You taught me that." Those words meant more to me than she'll ever know. Her fierce independence and passion for knowledge have taken her all over the world. She lives and works in Dubai...for now.

In high school, my son Daniel pushed himself to take part in a play in spite of his social phobia. It was there that a miracle happened...he found his voice. After high school, he moved back to New York City to pursue his dream of becoming an actor and was in several off-Broadway performances. But the highly competitive field of acting proved to be a disappointment. He still does public speaking as an interpretive guide at the September 11 Museum, and his interest in military history has inspired him to become a writer. He has published several articles in major military magazines and has a book in progress.

I will be the first to admit that I have not been the perfect parent, thus I give all credit to my children for having taken the bits of wisdom I have imparted and flown with them in the right direction. The glory is all theirs; the pride is mine.

Sadly, my sister Wanda and brother Edwin passed away from catastrophic illnesses. Mother passed away recently from old age, having lived a long and comfortable life under sister Bernadette's care. Brother Gilbert retired as a detective from the New York Police Department. He and his wife, Shirley, have shared an immutable spiritual bond that has transcended the sublime and the unexplainable. They are both breast cancer survivors.

Bernadette found the love of her life at the age of thirty-eight, proving that one should never give up hope on finding "the one." She and her husband, Brad, continue to provide a loving environment for her adopted children, Kristy and Christian.

Evelyn, Zoraida and I still stay in touch. It has been a loyal friendship that has spanned over twenty years of life's ebb and flow of joys and sorrows.

When Aimée was about twenty and Daniel fourteen, they received a call from Eron. Aimée went to visit him with my blessing. To this day, she will not discuss what transpired except to say that she regretted having gone and that she would not be communicating with him again. Perhaps it was a case of too little too late. They have not heard from him since.

There's something to be said about the power of forgiveness. It has been a liberating force in my life. I eventually came to understand that in harboring the anger, the bitterness and resentment towards those that had hurt me, I was giving the reins of control over to them. Forgiving was not about accepting their words and deeds. Forgiving was about letting go and moving on with my life. In doing so, I had finally set myself free.

Corrie Ten Boom, a holocaust survivor, said it most succinctly:

> "To forgive is to set the prisoner free
> and to realize
> that prisoner was me."